Natural Florida Landscaping

Dan Walton and Laurel Schiller

Pineapple Press, Inc.
Sarasota, Florida

Inquiries should be addressed to:

Pineapple Press, Inc.
P.O. Box 3889
Sarasota, Florida 34230

www.pineapplepress.com

Library of Congress Cataloging-in-Publication Data
  Library of Congress Cataloging-in-Publication Data

  Walton, Dan.
   Natural Florida landscaping / Dan Walton and Laurel Schiller. -- 1st ed.
     p. cm.
   ISBN-13: 978-1-56164-388-2 (pbk. : alk. paper)
   1. Natural landscaping--Florida. 2. Native plant gardening--Florida. I. Schiller, Laurel.
  II. Title.
   SB439.24.F6W35 2007
   635.9'51759--dc22

                                                                2007003982

First Edition
10 9 8 7 6 5 4 3

Printed in the United States of America

Contents

A color insert appears between pages 16 and 17.

Acknowledgments

We would like to acknowledge a number of people whose help has been gratefully received.

Cammie Donaldson for her advice, her encouragement, and her suggestions about the manuscript. She was always upbeat about the need for and usefulness of such a book. David Chiappini for suggestions about the manuscript and his photographs. Michael Ellison for his generosity as an editor. He transformed some of our more convoluted sentences into something approaching clarity. He was also one of our first clients to use native plants in a naturalistic way. Fran Palmeri for her tireless efforts, her skill in taking photographs, and her unflagging encouragement.

Friends of native plants who sent in photographs: We appreciate your generosity even though cost constraints did not allow us to use many of them. Anne Johnson, editor of the Pelican Press, for printing a number of our articles, which ultimately led to many of the chapters in this book.

Ellen Maloff for advocating a trees-first philosophy and for taking photographs. Jean Blackburn for her help on the Edible Gardening chapter and for taking photographs. Sally Webster for taking time to help us format the manuscript. Our partner Janice de Grineau for her commitment to the nursery. Finally, our thanks to June Cussen and Helena Berg of Pineapple Press for their final polishing. We thank all of the above. You helped to make this book a reality. Thanks to Bill Bissett, landscape architect for The Natives, Inc., for his landscape plan.

Introduction

This book is based on our ten years of growing and landscaping experience as native plant nursery owners. Our trial-and-error efforts to transform our yards, as well as those of numerous willing clients, provide the philosophical bases and design information that follow. It was from this work that we developed our interest in and appreciation for a more naturalistic approach to landscaping than is common in Florida. We have both enjoyed the transformation of our yards from sterile, lawn-dominated hot spaces into shady, plant-rich oases that we share with local wildlife.

As land is developed in Florida the native flora is being removed and too often replaced with vegetation not native to Florida. Several unfortunate consequences result from this removal. Wildlife habitat is reduced; water, fertilizer, and pesticide usage increases; the appearance of Florida is altered; and the natural balance of the environment is disturbed. For these reasons we believe urban and suburban dwellers must try to reduce the damage being done to our ecosystems by viewing our yards as part of the natural system. This means using native plants in our yards and doing it in a way more attuned to natural places. Our primary purpose in writing this book is to help Florida residents accomplish this.

As nursery owners, we have observed that people moving here from northern climates often become bewildered about gardening in Florida even though they were successful gardeners elsewhere. Our hot wet summers, the hot dry springs, the cool dry winters, the nutrient-poor sandy soils, the hardpan that can lead to water-logged soils in the summer—all these add up to a difficult environment for plants, particularly those not adapted to this region. Many folks, unfamiliar with these conditions, make poor plant choices when they move to Florida and often regret their selections after years of frustrated gardening. We discuss a variety of the problems that you may have to deal with and discuss the plants that can thrive in Florida's climate. We hope to help you make your plantings more successful, whether you are a new resident trying to plan your landscape or you have been here awhile and have begun to realize that using native plants would be easier for you and better for Florida.

Florida is a glorious place to garden and develop a natural landscape. We have a climate that enables you to garden almost all year-round and native plants that don't take decades to mature. You can have the joy of creating and watching an aesthetically pleasing, life-supporting landscape develop while also taking pleasure in the fact that it is environmentally sensitive.

1

Change Your Mindset

A Naturalistic and Environmentally Sensitive Approach

Our objective in this book is to show how you can create a native plant–filled yard that is naturalistic and can be maintained in an environmentally sensitive way.

The dictionary definition of naturalistic is "imitating nature closely." We don't suggest that your property can be indistinguishable from a natural area, unless you have had the good fortune to have your house built in a natural area with only a minimal effect on the vegetation during construction and later landscaping. Most of us have to deal with property from which the natural vegetation has been removed and replaced with plants foreign to our area.

By naturalistic we mean two things:

(1) Planting vegetation that is native to your region. By native we mean vegetation that was present in Florida at the time of European colonization (around 450 years ago).

(2) Planting in such a way that your yard looks as though it had grown from naturally dispersed seed rather than from carefully placed nursery stock. This will mean planting your yard in a more intensive, but less ordered, multilayered way similar to what you can see in

woodlands, rather than trying to create a more formal landscape with its symmetries and carefully located plant beds. To do this may require you to develop a new mindset about your yard and its landscaping.

Environmentally sensitive means, among other things, that you minimize the quantities of water, fertilizer, and pesticides that you use around your home. To accomplish this, you will need to reduce or remove your lawn and plant in its place a variety of native plants. Native plants, if properly selected, can thrive on rainfall after they have become established. Unlike turf grass they can thrive without fertilizer, as they have existed for eons on the nutrient-poor sandy Florida soils. Canopy trees and large shrubs and vines, when properly placed, can reduce energy use for air-conditioning by shading walls and windows. All plants, native or not, are subject to insect attack and fungal disease. In most cases, native plants will survive without pesticides, which can kill beneficial insects as well as harmful ones.

The increasing loss of natural habitat to urban development makes it important for homeowners to plant native species that will attract and maintain wildlife such as birds, butterflies, and other beneficial insects. We describe plants that are particularly useful to wildlife and how they can be used in your landscape.

Another aspect of environmentally sensitive gardening is growing your own fruits and vegetables. We discuss methods you can use to have a small vegetable and fruit garden. We know that a backyard gardener cannot grow everything needed to feed a family, but you can grow a considerable amount of fresh produce during the 8–10-month growing season we have in Florida. Energy savings are made when fruit and vegetables aren't shipped thousands of miles to market.

2
Rethinking Your Florida Yard

In its purest sense naturalistic would mean replacing your lawn and all of your exotic plants with natives that once grew where your house is now located. It would be as though your house were plunked down in the middle of pristine woodland, beach, or prairie. A less rigorous approach is to reduce your lawn, leave some exotics, and plant natives among them. If you leave exotics make sure they are not invasive and require neither irrigation nor fertilizer.

What Goes and What Stays

You have decided that you would like to begin to develop a more naturalistic landscape.

First, identify what you have. Go to your local library or bookstore and check out the Florida gardening section. You will find books on landscape plants and their care that will identify many of the plants found in the state. Gardening books that include information on your region will be most useful, since Florida has a number of growing zones based on the number of days below freezing. The internet also includes numerous websites that have pictures and descriptions of Florida plants. See the list of books and websites at the end of this book.

Take leaves of plants (fruit and flowers if they are available) you can't identify to your County Cooperative Extension office. Volunteers from their master gardener program will identify your plants. They also have a hotline and publications on everything from tropical ornamentals to native trees of Florida. Botanical gardens and retail garden centers are other places where plants are labeled. Identifying your plants is not as daunting an undertaking as you might think. You will be helped by the fact that many of the same landscape plants have been used over and over in Florida. Once you have identified the plants on your property, you are now ready to determine which should stay and which should go.

Keep the native plants. These are plants that are indigenous to Florida and adapted to our climate and soil conditions. They add life to your landscape by attracting birds, butterflies, and other wildlife. Native plants that are healthy and well-placed should stay. If you are building a new home and are lucky enough to have undisturbed natural areas on your property, preserve them. Tell your builder which plants must be saved if at all possible. Protect trees and shrubs with barriers. Existing vegetation will provide shade and buffers more quickly and less expensively than later planting.

Remove the invasive exotics. Exotics are species of plants that originate outside of Florida. Invasive exotics take over the landscape and displace native plants and animals. They include tropical houseplants, ground covers, and profusely seeding exotic shrubs and trees. A list of problematic plants is provided by the Florida Exotic Pest Plant Council at www.fleppc.org. Your County Cooperative Extension office can provide you with a list of plants to avoid in your area. If these plants occur on your property you should remove them. Learn their names and don't buy them.

A word of caution: Beware of friends and neighbors bearing gift plants. Neighbors give away plants that have done *too well* in their yards. A gift plant can do *too well* in your yard too. Don't accept plants from others until you understand their potential.

Keep houseplants indoors. Tropical houseplants replanted outdoors should go. It is amazing, and even wondrous, to come down from "The North" and see rubber plants, corn plants, and schefflera growing to enormous sizes when planted outside in the ground. You remember them as fragile plants you babied in your living room through the northern winter so that you had something green to look at. In Florida they quickly outgrow the outdoor spaces you have provided for them. Some of them are also invasive. Frosts may injure or kill them, creating reoccurring cleanup problems. They displace native plants that provide roosting sites and food for birds and other wildlife. There are better choices, so don't keep your predecessor's Norfolk Island pine, pothos, or philodendron.

Take out turf wherever you can. Turf grass does not do well in Florida without irrigation, fertilizer, and pesticides. These chemicals get into the ground water and then pollute our waterways. Mowing turf during the hot months is an expense to both energy and the pocketbook. Figure out how little turf you can live with, surround it with other plantings that will absorb the chemical runoff, and work toward eliminating it altogether.

Remove unsuitable trees. Many non-native, fast-growing, weedy trees such as Indian rosewood, chinaberry, jacaranda, Chinese tallowood, and *Ficus benjamina* have been planted in Florida landscapes. Although they were probably considered desirable by garden "experts" at the time they were planted, many are poorly suited to our soils or climate. In addition, they are often the most susceptible to hurricane damage. Removing unsuitable trees may be one of your early priorities.

Determine the condition of native trees on your property and whether they were properly placed. Sometimes homeowners place large shade trees too close to the foundation of the home in order to produce quick shade. Removing large shade trees is both heartbreaking and expensive. Call in a certified Florida arborist before making any decision about which trees should stay or go. These professionals know Florida trees and can determine the health of your trees.

You might consider planting native alternatives *before* you remove any undesirable trees. This gives you time to get a replacement established before you remove the original tree, particularly if it blocks an unsightly view or provides needed shade. Prune the undesirable tree to allow light, air, and moisture to reach its replacement, and slowly continue to thin it until your new tree is fully established. This may take three or four years of effort on your part, but it will make the transition period less stressful.

Sometimes a number of trees have been planted in a small space to create quick shade. This is all right if they are properly located. Go to a natural area and look at how trees grow in the woods. You'll see that many grow in groves. None of the individual trees grow as large as they would if growing in a more isolated situation. Oak hammocks, pine flatwoods, and coastal upland communities support numbers of closely growing trees.

Pull out problem shrubs. Existing shrubs are often problematic. The practice of planting against the foundation of the home is common here in Florida as elsewhere. This is a very hostile place for plants. Under the eaves there is little moisture, space, or air circulation. Poor quality "fill" soils are often imported from off site to raise the house above the flood plain. In time you will end up with sickly shrubs that have been severely pruned to keep them away from the walls and below the windows. If they are woody with little foliage it is best to remove them.

Shrubs, no matter where they occur on your property, can suffer from woefully ignorant trimming rituals used to maintain a preconceived idea of what the shrubs should look like and how large they should grow. Many existing shrubs are not worth keeping because severe pruning has damaged them. The resulting stress to the plant may also have resulted in disease and pest problems. Get rid of all diseased, pest-infested shrubs, but don't be concerned if some of your plants have leaf spots or insect galls. These may be somewhat unsightly but are not usually harmful. You may want to try to get rid of the infestations with a few weekly spraying cycles with oil or soap sprays. Often the problem is that the shrub is *the wrong plant in the wrong place,* and the infestations and diseases will recur.

Make sure that your shrubs are drought tolerant and can exist on rainfall. If you are irrigating shrubs, wean them slowly from your system over a two- or three-month period. At the end of this time assess the health and vigor of the shrubs. If they are not able to adjust and require hand watering between periods of rainfall they should be removed.

Get ground covers under control. Some non-native and native ground covers and vines can be very aggressive. Folks plant these as fast growers to cover a lot of ground or fencing. Often they do much more. They grow over everything, smothering shrubs and flower beds as well as climbing into and over trees. Many are difficult to control once they get started. They spread so rapidly during our long growing season that keeping them within bounds can be a never-ending nightmare. Remove these plants from your property before you plant anything else. It is easier to get rid of existing problematic ground covers and vines before they overtake new plants.

Be choosy with flower beds. Flowers, like all other types of plants have light, moisture, and soil requirements. If you have flower beds, you need to determine whether they are in locations that will provide what the plants need. If you are thinking of planting new beds, make sure that they also will be in good locations. Color coordination is attractive, but if the plants are not in the right locations they will not thrive. Focus on a mixture of native reseeding annuals and perennials.

Summary. Remove invasive exotics, houseplants, and poorly placed sickly shrubs and trees. Begin to reduce or eliminate turf. What remains should be well-placed and thrive without irrigation, fertilizer, or pesticides—and should appeal to you.

Why Native Plants?

In a more perfect world, developers and builders would remove the absolute minimum number of native plants from a building site. This has rarely been done in the past, nor does it seem likely in the future. Consequently, instead of a landscape that has developed *in situ* without attention, pampered nursery-grown plants are brought in to landscape properties that have been considerably altered from their original state. In most instances these plants are not indigenous to Florida, i.e., they are not native.

Plants native to Florida have adapted to our climate, which combines cool dry winters, hot dry springs, and hot humid summers. They have also adapted to the nutrient-poor sandy soils that are either excessively drained or waterlogged after heavy rains. Coastal native plants are able to tolerate salt-laden winds and soils. In addition, native trees have evolved to withstand tropical storm–force winds, and some can even endure hurricane-force winds.

These adaptations enable appropriate native plants in your landscape to thrive year-round on rainfall without supplemental water, no matter how far apart the rains might be. Once established, you will not need to water the plants again. As indicated above, native plants have adapted to nutrient-poor soils and consequently do not require supplemental fertilization to thrive. Healthy native plants can generally tolerate insect attack and diseases caused by microorganisms without the use of pesticides.

Native plants support populations of native fauna including birds, butterflies, and a wide variety of crucially important insect pollinators. At the Archbold Biological Station in southern Florida, 294 different insect species were observed visiting the flowers of saw palmetto plants. Various studies have shown that plants in different parts of the world attract a multitude of insects when planted in their native locations, but when introduced to exotic locations they attract only a small number. Insects are food sources for birds and other wildlife, as well as pollinators, and the replacement of native plants with introduced ones can disrupt many food chains. As more wild land is developed, urban and suburban yards planted with natives will become increasingly important sources of food and shelter for wildlife.

A less obvious, but significant, role for native plants in urban areas is the aesthetic. We develop our sense of place in part from the native trees and flowers we see around us, even if we don't know their identities. One of the ways we recognize we are in Florida and not in Ohio, other than the absence of winter snow, is the presence of massive live oaks, stately slash pines, and cabbage palms, as well as other less well-known plants. Non-native plants may have their place amongst our urban spaces, but surely the replacement of our native flora with exotics is comparable to replacing our native birds with species of parrots because we enjoy their colorful plumage.

Another reason to be careful about non-native plants is that they may be invasive species that have the potential to replace native flora in natural areas well as in your yard. Millions of dollars are spent each year in Florida killing exotics that have been introduced without realizing their invasive qualities.

Natural Groupings of Native Plants

Customers at our nursery often say they are interested in native plants because they have found that many of their non-native plants were short-lived and thus had to be replaced often. In selecting native plants for your landscape, however, keep in mind that a particular native plant also may not thrive everywhere. As is the case for all plants, native plants must be planted in the right place with regard to soil moisture, light, shade, etc.

Some natives will thrive in your landscape while others won't. Why? The answer is that the ones that thrive are probably a part of the natural grouping of natives that once grew in what is now your yard. The soils around your foundation may be imported fill dirt used to raise your home above the flood plain. However, ten to fifteen feet away from your home's foundation the soils are probably those that were part of the original local ecosystem in your area, whether pine flatwoods, oak hammock, beach dune, or coastal upland. The soil characteristics and microclimate will favor certain native plant communities over others. You can recreate a natural plant community by planting the major canopy trees and understory plants that once grew there. To get an idea of what type of vegetation was originally in your area, visit undisturbed lots or parks with native habitat. Look up local ecosystem maps in books on Florida ecology.

Much of Florida was once covered with pine flatwoods. Remnant old pines or stands of pines may still exist in your neighborhood if your area was originally this type of habitat. Pines grow in both well-drained and poorly drained soils with a subsurface hardpan. You need to know which conditions are present in your yard because different understory plants grow in dry or wet soils.

Coastal sites must obviously include a species mix that does well in areas of salt water inundation or spray. Coastal areas also have milder climates and thus a different combination of plants than areas farther inland. Inland areas were most likely either pine flatwoods or wetter areas of mesic hammocks.

The following list gives typical plant groupings for three of the most common plant communities in Florida:

Coastal Upland

Canopy Trees: southern red cedar, southern magnolia, red bay, sand live oak, sabal palm, gumbo limbo, sugarberry

Understory Trees: fiddlewood, stoppers, palms, sea grape, wild lime, holly

Shrubs: beautyberry, coral bean, yaupon holly, wax myrtle, saw palmetto, wild coffee, cocoplum, myrsine, Florida privet, marlberry, firebush

Pine Flatwoods

Canopy Trees: slash pine, longleaf pine, sabal palm

Understory Trees: holly, red bay

Shrubs: beautyberry, cocoplum, wax myrtle, myrsine, saw palmetto, grasses

Mesic Hardwood Forest

Canopy Trees: Florida maple, sweet gum, magnolia, oaks, elms, bald cypress, sabal palm, holly

Understory Trees: redbud, holly, mulberry, plum, cherry laurel, dogwood

Shrubs: firebush, wild coffee, yellow anise, marlberry, wax myrtle, viburnum, saw palmetto, grasses

It is not necessary to plant only what might have grown naturally in your yard. Planting all natives is not even necessary. You need to plant what *can* grow in your yard without irrigation, fertilization, and pesticide application. By choosing plants that could have grown there originally, you will be definitely choosing hardy material adapted to your landscape.

Reduce Your Lawn

Formal lawns were popularized in Britain beginning in the 18th century. In that country of mild climate and evenly spread rainfall, grass does amazingly well. The British penchant for lawns was brought to this country, where in the Northeast and some other parts of the country, grass also can thrive. Estimates are that more than 25 million acres are now planted in residential lawns in the U.S. Unfortunately, lawns have been planted in areas of the country where they do not thrive without supplemental irrigation, fertilizer, and pesticides. The desert Southwest is one example and Florida is another.

Florida has a climate that includes both warm/dry and hot/wet cycles. The sandy soils do not retain moisture and are not naturally fertile. Consequently, grass does not do well unless irrigated during warm dry periods and fertilized and treated with pesticides. Water, fertilizer, and pesticides have become increasingly expensive to the homeowner, and perhaps more importantly, expensive to the environment. Estimates are that Americans spend $17 billion on their lawns including everything from pesticides to lawn tractors. It is estimated that 50% of the household water used in Florida is for irrigating the lawns, that make up 80% to 90% of properties not covered with buildings. For example, in Sarasota, on the southwest coast, studies have shown that most of the nitrogen ending up in Phillipi Creek, which runs into Sarasota Bay, comes from fertilized lawns rather than from the septic tanks that surround the creek.

Many homeowners are not willing to irrigate and fertilize and, consequently, their lawns are mostly weedy sand patches that are brown for months during the dry season. Nevertheless, they still have to mow them or have them mowed. This process itself is costly both to the homeowner and to the environment. The amount of gasoline burned in mowers (estimated to be over 300 million gallons in the U.S.) adds to urban air and noise pollution. Estimates are that a typical lawn mower emits more than ten times as much polluting hydrocarbon as the average car per hour of use.

All of the above are good reasons for you to consider reducing the area of grass surrounding your house. Some folks decide to go for broke and remove their entire lawn in one shot. Most people prefer to reduce their lawns gradually. A simple way to begin is to remove grass from under any existing trees and shrubs out to their drip lines and then mulch this area. This reduces the grassed area and trees and shrubs will grow better, since they won't have to compete with the grass for water and nutrients. Think about which areas of your lawn can be converted to other plantings such as trees, shrubs, clump grasses, flower beds, or low ground covers. Consider shading the south and west sides of your house with trees or tall shrubs. The west side of your house particularly needs shading to reduce the heating of your house by the late afternoon sun. In addition, driveways should be shaded so that getting into your car on a summer's day becomes less of an ordeal. Are there areas that would benefit by using shrubs as a screen?

We suggest that you draw up a plan for gradually removing your grass and replacing it with other plants. Figure out the smallest amount of lawn you can live with. Use a drought-tolerant grass such as bahia. Don't use St. Augustine because it requires irrigation to look good. As we mentioned, you can't have a uniformly green lawn without fertilizing and using pesticides. If you use these chemicals, surround your grass with other mulched native plantings to intercept stormwater runoff that will carry the chemicals into the storm sewers and then into waterways. The pesticides used on your lawn can be injurious to humans, as well as birds and butterflies. If you do fertilize, use slow-release forms. Start with half the amount and apply it half as often as recommended by the manufacturer. No matter how well you treat your lawn, don't expect it to look good for more than three or fours years without major rehabilitation.

How to Kill the Grass and Associated Weeds

There are basically three ways to kill grass and associated weeds: a.) light-blocking, b.) mechanical, c.) chemical. To do a thorough job, you will often need to combine at least two of these methods.

Light-blocking. Whether or not you use light-blocking to kill grass and weeds you will need it in some form to help keep them out once they have been initially removed. Light-blockers (mulches) come in many forms, both organic and inorganic. They vary from chopped bark, leaves, newspapers, and peanut hulls to stones, lava rock, and shells. We recommend organic mulches. Stone and shell are better used for pathways and parking areas.

Eliminating turf using only mulch is difficult. Spreading old rugs or black plastic over a small area of lawn for two to three weeks can be effective, but you must be sure that the grass is dead. If you see green under the dead brown grass on the surface it means that the kill is not complete and you should continue the treatment. Several inches of newspaper under a three-inch layer of mulch will increase the effectiveness of the mulch while allowing moisture to reach the soil. The paper will last four to eight months before it is completely degraded. On slopes the loss of mulch from the surface will expose the newspaper which is not aesthetically pleasing. Killing turf by using the mulch/newspaper combination without other treatment is possible, but a prior treatment with a glyphosate-containing herbicide as discussed below will ensure success.

Landscape Fabric. These are woven or nonwoven fabrics that prevent light from reaching the soil while allowing water and fertilizer to pass. Mulch is spread over top of the fabric for aesthetic reasons and to retard the fabric's decomposition. You can plant through the fabric by slicing openings in it. It functions like newspaper, and although much more expensive, lasts longer. As is the case for newspapers, the loss of mulch results in unsightly exposed plastic areas.

Trees and Shrubs. Shade produced by trees and shrubs will reduce grass and weed growth as the plants mature. Shade will be most effective if you do not irrigate the plants, since without added water, they will effectively compete with grass and most weeds for soil moisture. Do not rake and bag the leaves because they will add a natural mulch. If you mulch the area around the trees or shrubs out to the drip line, this combination will be highly effective in reducing weeds. Keep the mulch about 6 inches from tree trunks because it will retain moisture that can lead to root rot problems. Remove the grass inside the drip line of trees with an herbicide or light-blocker. Do not dig up the turf since this may damage the feeder roots.

Mechanical. Digging up the grass has the disadvantage of providing ideal conditions for the weed seed already in the soil to germinate. The major advantage is that the soil is loosened. If you are dealing with a soil that contains a considerable amount of clay or one that is compacted, there may be advantages to digging up the turf. If you do dig, wait several weeks until the weed seeds have germinated and then either use a light blocker or spot-treat the area with an herbicide.

Chemical. Glyphosate-containing formulations such as Roundup have become the classic herbicides used to kill most unwanted plant material. The herbicide is sprayed on the leaves and translocated to the roots where it kills the plant. One of the advantages of glyphosate is that it inhibits a specific enzyme found only in plants and microorganisms so its toxicity is low in animals, including humans, birds, insects, and fish. In addition to glyphosate, Roundup contains a surfactant that is irritating to the skin and eyes. Keep it away from ponds and streams as there is evidence that Roundup can be toxic to amphibians such as frogs and fish. There are formulations such as Rodeo for aquatic use that do not contain the surfactant used in Roundup. Since Roundup is toxic to almost all plants, care must be taken with its use. This means that spraying should be done on a calm day so wind-borne spray doesn't reach plants not meant to be killed. If you accidentally spray an unintended plant, quickly rinse it with copious amounts of water.

Roundup is formulated so that a few hours after spraying it is not affected by rain. Complete killing requires seven to ten days and a second spraying of missed areas is usually necessary. After the grass is dead do not dig it up or you will be negating the principal advantage of using an herbicide. Freshly dug soil is weed seed heaven. Plant into the dead vegetation by digging holes only large enough for the new plant material. Mulch the entire treated area, including the dead grass.

Roundup and other glyphosate-containing herbicides can be obtained from garden centers either as concentrated or dilute solutions. The concentrated solutions are diluted and applied with a garden sprayer, and the dilute solutions come in a small container and can be applied directly.

1. Beach dune sunflowers line an inviting mulched path from the front to the back yard. Maintenance involves occasionally pruning this fast-growing annual ground cover off the path and removing older woody plants every year or so to encourage seedlings to take their place. (Fran Palmeri)

2. Low areas between properties provide ample room to plant wetland and wetland-edge native plants. These plants thrive in areas that are frequently inundated with water during the summer months but dry most of the winter. Fall-blooming grasses such as muhly grass and bluestems grow beneath sweet bay, magnolia, maple, and cypress trees. Large firebush, wax myrtle, and Walter's viburnum produce nectar, berries, and seeds for resident and migratory birds and butterflies. (Fran Palmeri)

3. Clump grasses such as this dwarf blue-green fakahatchee grass and surrounding perennial peanut are excellent substitutes for sod. In full sun or partial shade, both are hardy and will thrive on rainfall alone without the use of commercial fertilizers or pesticides, which pollute local waterways. (Fran Palmeri)

4. The native plantings in this front yard muffle the sounds of a busy coastal street. The owners look out at firebush, fiddlewood, myrsine, marlberry, and silver buttonwood instead of streaming cars. This naturalistic planting is an excellent substitute for a high wall or fence that would block the cooling sea breezes. (Fran Palmeri)

5. Red salvia and yellow flowering senna shrubs will draw butterflies to this patio edge for up-close viewing pleasure. The flowers of these plants are nectar sources for adult butterflies. Female sulphur butterflies, such as the barred yellow and cloudless sulphur, seek out senna plants to lay eggs on; the plants will later provide food for the caterpillar stage. It is necessary to have both nectar and larval food plants if you wish to attract a wide range of butterflies to your yard. (Fran Palmeri)

6. Much of Florida was once covered by pine flatwoods. Pines grow quickly and provide the high, light shade most plants prefer. Pine needles break down quickly and acidify the soil. Covering the ground with a layer of pine straw will keep moisture around the roots of newly planted specimens and reduce watering time and cost during the establishment period. Pine straw mulch looks woodsy and inviting and smells wonderful underfoot. By planting pines on their property, these homeowners have blended their homesite with the surrounding pine woodlands. (Fran Palmeri)

7. Postage-stamp-sized front entranceways can provide attractive native plantscapes rather than sterile places filled with stressed exotics struggling to survive in too-wet or too-dry conditions. Here, St. Francis holds out a tray-style bird feeder surrounded by hardy native grasses and wildflowers in and amongst attractive containers. The native ground cover flowing out onto the path is mimosa, which has its pink flower pom-poms from March to December. (Fran Palmeri)

8. Small side yards need not be neglected places to store bikes, lumber, or lawn furniture. At this home an inviting shell path winds between water features and ornamental pots amongst native plants that thrive in the shade. Wild coffee, marlberry, numerous kinds of ferns, fakahatchee grass, ground covers such as prostrate porterweed and red salvia, as well as low-growing native palms such as needle palm or *Sabal minor,* do well in constrained locations. (Fran Palmeri)

9. Instead of lawn grass, plant a variety of tall and low-growing shrubs such as the coontie, shown here, beneath and around your shade trees to provide a woodland appearance and minimize maintenance. Don't rake up the leaves but let them add to the commercial mulch you may have originally spread. (Fran Palmeri)

10. Muscadine grapes are relished by wildlife and homeowners. Train them up over a gazebo or lattice roof for privacy, quick shade, and enjoyable eating. In tall trees they provide cover for nesting birds. Prune vine stalks at ground level to control growth. (Fran Palmeri)

11. Brambles provide color and interest in the native garden as well as edible fruit. There are many kinds to choose from such as sawtooth blackberry (*Rubus argutus*), sand blackberry (*Rubus cuneifolius*), and northern and southern dewberry (*R. flagellaris* and *R. trivialis,* respectively). Their thorny branches shelter ground-nesting birds from cats and snakes. (Fran Palmeri)

12. Tuck pineapple plants into sunny to partly sunny garden beds as an edible ground cover. They grow easily in our sandy soils and each plant will produce a golden pineapple in eighteen months. The spiky plant fronds provide contrast and texture in landscape beds. Cooling shade comes from massive laurel and live oaks, which shade the west and south sides of this home on larger acreage. (Jean Blackburn)

13. Tropical native plants can be showy accents as well as ample nectar sources for migratory ruby-throated hummingbirds or resident butterflies. Once established this trouble-free eight- to ten-foot native firebush shrub will bloom non-stop most of the year. It can be grown as an annual in the northern half of the state. (Fran Palmeri)

14. Jacquemontia, or Everglades morning glory, blooms almost all year in southern Florida. Its delicate periwinkle flowers cover a trellis quickly. Trellises provide privacy in small areas such as side yards where there isn't room for shrubs or fill in temporarily while larger plants grow. (Fran Palmeri)

15. A major reason for planting a native yard is to create a haven for local wildlife such as this female cardinal. She requires a sturdily branched shrub to nest in and berries, seeds, and insects to feed her young. (Fran Palmeri)

16. We seldom use the outer fifteen to twenty feet of our back yards. Surround your private spaces with a buffer of native trees, shrubs, and palms that also provide wildlife habitat. Plant in groupings two to three plants wide for a dense, diverse, and fast fill-in. Resist hedging. The planting shown here buffers a single-family home from a large, ugly, hot asphalt parking lot. (Ellen Maloff)

17. Runoff from fertilized, pesticide-treated lawns and landscapes pollutes our waterways. Don't use toxic chemicals. Remove the outer ten to fifteen feet of your lawn and create a chemical-free buffer of mulched native plants between your home and storm drains, retention ponds, and creeks. Smaller shrubs and ground covers along the curb or clump grasses and reseeding native wildflowers along a ditch, as pictured here, will absorb runoff before it leaves your property. (Fran Palmeri)

18. Not much blooms in the shade of oaks, but Florida beautyberry produces delicate pink flowers in summer and purple porcelain-like berries in the fall. Mockingbirds cherish them, as do cardinals and blue jays. These berries hang on long after the leaves have dropped off and can be used in flower arrangements if hung to dry. Take a walk in your local woods and see what else grows under oaks and then buy native nursery specimens to create a naturalized landscape area in your yard. (Fran Palmeri)

19. This homeowner protected the natural buffer behind construction barricades while his home was built. From his screened lanai he looks out on cedar, scrub oak, pine, and assorted understory plants such as wild coffee, myrsine, viburnum, and saw palmetto. He told us he enjoys looking at greenery and birds and not into his neighbor's pool cage. (Fran Palmeri)

20. A grove of smaller trees, such as these scrub oaks, can take the place of one large shade tree. Florida holly, dwarf magnolia, viburnum, myrtle, and sabal palm can also be used. In their shade plant saw palmetto, native ferns, and grasses. (Fran Palmeri)

21. A small water garden is a feasible and inexpensive weekend project in Florida. Create this oasis near an office window or off your lanai where you can enjoy the beauty of aquatic water lilies and other pond plants, listen to the calls of frogs, and marvel at the iridescent shine of dragonflies. Cheap, store-bought, live-bearing minnows will eat mosquito larvae. It is possible to create a natural pond without a pump and filters by using plants wisely. (Fran Palmeri)

22. Brilliant red berries from a wild coffee plant are a welcoming sight along this walk from the driveway to front door. Scrub oaks create shade and a woodlands feel to this entrance way. (Fran Palmeri)

3

Create a
Naturalistic
Plan

Creating a plan for your yard that looks naturalistic requires considerable thought. We are not talking about buying a variety of native plants and haphazardly planting them around your home wherever space allows. We are also not advocating that you just stop mowing and pruning and let nature take its course.

The best place to start is to visit nearby natural areas. Get a feel for what native plants thrive in your area. Notice what kinds of trees grow there, what shrubs, native grasses, wildflowers, and vines. Once you can recognize the major kinds of native plants, look at how they are naturally spaced. Note what trees dominate and what types of shrubs are common. Note how grasses, vines, and wildflowers are scattered throughout the area. Look at the patterns of light and shade, high and low ground, and recognize that native species of plants, like all plants, have unique needs and that species composition changes as the amount of sunlight, drainage, moisture, and soil characteristics change.

Next, walk around your property with a fresh, clear mental picture of the natural areas you visited. What aspects of native Florida would you like to re-create around your home? Do you want to create the cool quiet feel of a shaded woodland with a mulch and natural leaf litter understory? Perhaps you would like to screen views with a dense thicket of mixed height native shrubs along the side or back property line? This buffer would provide nesting opportunities for local wildlife, a priority for some homeowners. Is there a low spot for a small pond or herbaceous mix of wetland plants?

Thinking about the aesthetics of your site also involves thinking about how much open space you would like in the front and back yards. Open space is often thought of as lawn, and indeed some homeowner associations require a minimum amount of turf. However, open space can also be mulch, shell, sand, or ground cover, depending on what uses you envision for it. Think through what you want to do on your property and develop a plan that fits your needs. In the trade this is called "let form follow function."

Once you have decided what you would like your yard to look like based on how you would like to use the spaces around your home, you need to think about how much you want to tackle at once. In an established landscape, you will need to decide what should stay and what should go in each area you want to work on. We discuss this in detail in the previous section on evaluating your landscape. Some folks will want to start small and make gradual changes over time. Others, on small lots or building a new home, can create a more natural plan all at one time.

Start with trees. Decide where you want them. The shade they create over time will determine where you plant shade-loving vs. sun-loving plants. Next, decide how much open space you want and where you want it. Everything else is available planting space. Give consideration to the following elements of design when thinking through your plan.

Color. In nature and in a naturalistic yard, a little color goes a long way. Seasonal wildflowers, summer-blooming shrubs, and colorful berries in the fall all provide color that is sparing but attractive. Every plant in your Florida yard does not have to be ever-blooming. This does not happen in nature and it will be much more exciting and less garish if it doesn't happen in your yard either. Group combinations of trees, shrubs, wildflowers, and vines according to their soil, moisture, and light requirements and not by color.

Shrubs provide predictable periods of color that last through the years. Wildflowers add ephemeral color for shorter time periods. White shows up well in shady areas. Think about leaf and frond colors. Native plants provide species of many hues including shades of green from silver-blue to chartreuse as well as reds and shades of purple.

Line and Balance. These design elements refer to how your eye moves around your property, what you notice and why. Naturalistic plantings should be nonlinear and asymmetrical. We might intuitively want to plant ordered, evenly spaced, linear arrangements. Yet "Nature abhors a straight line." Strive to create curved paths through slightly randomized plantings. Two of anything creates the appearance of soldiers at attention, so plant odd numbers. Straight walks to front doors, straight driveways to large garages, and straight paths to backyards add artificial structure and detract from the natural feel of native plantings.

Form and Texture. These elements create interest in native plantings. They are much more important than plant color in a naturalistic setting. Native trees have beautiful forms that spread or climb skyward. Leaf and frond texture, form, and size create interesting contrasts in the more subtle naturalistic landscape. You are more aware of smooth or rough and glossy or dull surfaces when you are not distracted by pervasive color. Contrasting shrub shapes, such as upright, weeping or horizontal, are more noticeable and pleasurable in a native yard.

Scale and Proportion. These are not major concerns in a naturalistic yard. Plantings will be site-appropriate and functional. In Florida, canopy trees grow very large, as do many native shrubs. Plant them where they will have space to grow and will not need to be severely pruned. Shade trees eventually grow much larger than a typical single-story home. Their beauty will soften and mask unattractive homes.

Unity, Rhythm, Repetition, Focus. Fitting all parts of your yard together may or may not be important to you. Some folks like rooms within rooms both indoors and outdoors. They create hidden surprises and spaces as they plan their yard. Others may wish to have everything flow together in a more uniform manner. Both types of design are possible in a naturalistic yard. Outdoor "rooms" can be created by strategically spacing larger native shrubs along meandering paths. To tie plantings together, pick several kinds of small shrubs, grasses, ground covers, and wildflowers and use them repeatedly. This is what one often observes in nature.

Examples of Naturalistic Plans

The essentials are simple. Plant a number of appropriate native trees, plan for your functional open spaces, and fill the rest of your yard with suitable native shrubs, grasses, vines, and wildflowers. A formal design is not a prerequisite but can provide a level of comfort. Here are two plans that give you visual representations of naturalistic yards. There can be many variations on these plans depending on your yard shape and size as well as on your own sense of aesthetics.

Landscape Plan for Your Florida Yard — 1

North

1 - Longleaf pine
2 - Red cedar
3 - Magnolia
4 - Live oak
5 - Winged elm
6 - Redbud
7 - River birch
8 - Crab apple
9 - Sabal palm
10 - Red bay

A - Beautyberry
B - Wax myrtle
C - Walter's viburnum
D - Anise
E - Oakleaf hydrangea
H - Hummingbird &
    Butterfly Garden
K - Holly

Central

1 - Slash pine or
    Longleaf pine
2 - Red cedar
3 - Magnolia
4 - Live oak
5 - Winged elm
6 - Yaupon holly
7 - River birch
8 - Firebush
9 - Sabal palm
10 - Red bay

A - Beautyberry
B - Wax myrtle
C - Walter's viburnum
D - Anise
E - Oakleaf hydrangea
H - Hummingbird &
    Butterfly Garden
K - Holly

South

1 - Slash pine or
    Longleaf pine
2 - Red cedar
3 - Mahogany
4 - Live oak
5 - Red maple
6 - Tamarind
7 - any Stopper
8 - Firebush
9 - Sabal palm
10 - Red bay

A - Beautyberry
B - Wax myrtle
C - Marlberry
D - Wild coffee
E - Necklace pod
H - Hummingbird &
    Butterfly Garden
K - Holly

] Depending on your needs this area would be your high-traffic space. Use ground cover, mulch, shell, or lawn.

] Mass plantings of low growing shrubs, ferns, coontie, or native clump grasses.

] Tree and shrub beds containing leaf litter, mulch, and ground cover.

A 24" boundary of shell, sand or stone should be left between your home and plantings.

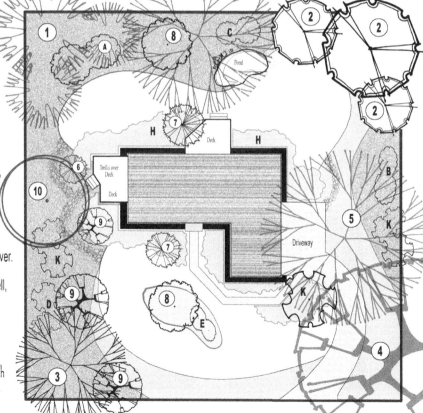

North

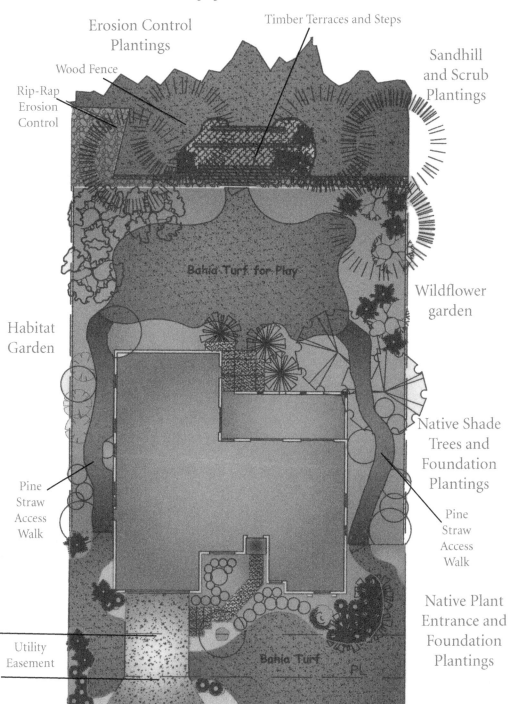

Erosion Control
Plantings

Timber Terraces and Steps

Sandhill
and Scrub
Plantings

Wood Fence

Rip-Rap
Erosion
Control

Bahia Turf for Play

Wildflower
garden

Habitat
Garden

Native Shade
Trees and
Foundation
Plantings

Pine
Straw
Access
Walk

Pine
Straw
Access
Walk

Native Plant
Entrance and
Foundation
Plantings

Utility
Easement

Bahia Turf

PL

Landscape for Your Florida Yard — 2

Erosion Control Plantings
Sunshine Mimosa
Purple Love Grass
Saw Palmetto
Carolina Jessamine

Habitat Garden
Coral Honeysuckle
Wax Myrtle
Myrtle Oak
Simpson's Stopper
Firebush
Carolina Aster
Coral Bean
Sumac

Native Plant Entrance and Foundation Plantings
Sabal Palm
Walter's Viburnum
Doghobble
Pink Muhly Grass
Dwarf Walter's Viburnum
St. John's Wort
Pineland Lantana
Coontie
Sand Cordgrass
Saw Palmetto

Sandhill and Scrub Plantings
Longleaf Pine
Summer Hawthorn
Saw Palmetto
Chickasaw Plum
Paw Paw
Wiregrass
Little Blueberry
Silver Buckthorn
Garberia
Rusty Lyonia

Wildflower garden
Blazing Star
Little White Ageratina
Twin Flower
Florida Paintbrush
Penstemon
Palafoxia
Sandhill Wireweed
Tropical Sage

Native Shade Trees and Foundation Plantings
Winged Elm
Florida Privet
Saw Palmetto
Firebush
Yaupon Holly
Simpson's Stopper

Shade Your Home

You can utilize trees and shrubs to shade your house from our long months of intense sun, yet allow the sun to warm it during cooler months. Canopy trees (trees that produce considerable shade) will shade your home's roof and walls and decrease air-conditioning costs through the hottest months of the year (May–September). It has been estimated that trees can reduce air-conditioning costs by 25% to 40%. They will also cool the outside air temperature by up to ten degrees and allow you to leave your windows open longer in the spring and reopen them sooner in the fall. Deciduous canopy trees (trees that lose their leaves in the winter) give the advantage of summer shade yet allow the sun to warm the walls and roof during the winter months. They are especially advantageous on the south side of your home since the winter sun is low in the southern sky and much of its warmth will come from that direction. The leafless branches of deciduous trees will allow the sun through to brighten and warm your south-facing rooms.

Ideally, you should plant shade trees around the entire perimeter of your house to produce shade throughout the day. If space is not available, maximize the benefits of shade trees by planting them on the west and south sides of your house. They will shade the building mass from the afternoon sun and reduce the buildup of heat over the course of the day. Do not remove a shade tree's lower branches since they effectively block the searing late afternoon sunlight that floods through the windows on the west or northwest side of your home.

We often hear comments from customers at our nursery that they are reluctant to plant a canopy tree because they won't see the benefits in their lifetime. If you plant canopy trees such as live oak, laurel oak, Florida elm, or maple when they are ten to twelve feet high, they can grow into twenty-five-foot shade trees in four to six years. They will continue to grow and produce shade and add both beauty and economic value to your property as well as to your neighborhood.

Driveways and concrete pool areas become large heat sinks in the summer months. The interior of your car will become broiling hot when the car is left on an unshaded driveway. If you plant evergreen trees such as conifers or hollies next to the driveway or pool area, you will have fewer problems with shedding leaves. Since these are slower-growing trees, it will probably take about six years before your driveway or pool area is partially shaded.

Large shrubs (six to twelve feet tall) and smaller trees (to about eighteen feet) can also effectively shade outside walls. On the east side they will block the early morning summer sun, and on the south and west sides, the full force of the afternoon and early evening sun. Both should be planted at least six to eight feet away from the edge of the foundation to give them ample room to grow and take advantage of natural rainfall. Young shrubs of sea grape, cocoplum, wax myrtle, yaupon holly, Walter's viburnum, Florida privet, firebush, or Simpson's stopper will grow tall enough to shade sidewalls in two or three seasons. Small trees such as dahoon holly, little gem magnolia, or sea grape (trained as a tree) will also provide shade in two or three seasons.

Do not plant vines to climb up your walls or place trellis work or strings against the walls and train vines on them. The vegetation will trap moisture on your walls and foundation that can lead to fungal infections. Vegetation so close to the home may attract insect pests that can cause structural damage to the building. It also encourages pests to enter your home in search of food and shelter. Vines on walls also make it impossible to paint or wash your walls.

Vines can be used to create shade when trained on a trellis. They are especially effective placed several feet from the sides of your home where there is not enough room to plant taller-growing shrubs and small trees. Build these at least two feet inside your property line so that the vines will not flow over the top and through the lattice onto your neighbor's property. Vines will climb up and through it by the end of the first or second growing season.

During the summer months the air conditioning unit should be shaded to maximize its cooling potential. Plant a large shrub or small tree on the west side of the unit. A trellis and vine can do the same thing in a limited space.

If you have a sidewalk in front of your house, try to plant a tree or trees that will shade it. We desperately need shaded sidewalks in Florida to encourage more people to walk. Even if you don't have a sidewalk, plant a canopy tree to shade the street in front of your home.

Garden for Wildlife

When you plant native plants you add life to your landscape by creating a haven on your property for wildlife. This is about living with and supporting nature around our homes. It is the opposite of having a landscape dominated by a lawn and a few palms or shrubs that will be a sterile space for wildlife.

We have the extra joy here of supporting not only diverse populations of resident wildlife but also migratory species that pass through Florida on their way to southern winter and northern summer ranges. This makes us an especially important wildlife corridor as well as homeland.

Gardening for wildlife requires using native plants in your landscape. Native plants have been growing here for thousands of years and are the natural food, shelter, and nesting plants of our local wildlife. Native plants and native wildlife have evolved together in an intricate food web. Birds, lizards, toads, frogs, foxes, butterflies, etc., may use exotic plantings as alternative food sources or resting sites and hiding places. However, they search out native plants for predictable sources of nectar, berries, insects, and firm branches in which to construct their nests.

Wildlife needs food, shelter, nesting or denning sites, and fresh water. To support many kinds of wildlife you will need to create many different kinds of wildlife niches on your property. Fairly sunny open areas protected from wind are ideal locations for butterfly gardens. Nectar-producing native flowers are necessary for butterflies and they need species-specific native plants as food for their caterpillars.

Migratory hummingbirds will seek nectar in sunny to fairly shady areas where they can find masses of mostly tubular blooms. Observe and learn about the diversity of other types of pollinating insects that will be attracted to your plants. These include many different kinds of bees, wasps, and moths. Plant these specialty gardens where you can readily view the interactions between host plants and the wildlife they attract. Great sites to consider include outside an office or kitchen window or near a sunny Florida room.

Most other birds, as well as resident wildlife, prefer to shelter, nest, and rear their young in undisturbed places in your yard. Provide these areas by killing the grass and planting a fifteen- to twenty-foot buffer around the periphery of your backyard. This area should include trees ground covers, grasses, and vines, as well as different kinds of shrubs of all sizes that provide seeds and berries. Make sure some of your shrubs are larger with strong, stiff branch angles to support nests and provide hiding places from the ground up. This shrub layer, or middle story layer, is probably the most important part of your naturalized border because wildlife utilize it the most. Allow this area to become dense, perhaps overgrown, and definitely neglected. The last thing a pair of nesting cardinals wants is someone out there every other week taming the wilderness by pruning, shaping, thinning, and weeding.

Make sure each area of your landscape connects with the others. By this we mean that there should be enough lower and middle story plantings to provide a sheltered corridor for lizards, frogs, small mammals, and other wildlife to move about freely from area to area without being disturbed by you or picked off by a predator. Create woodpiles and brushy thickets in which critters can hide. This is especially important for those species that don't fly. Nesting rabbits, native mice, and perhaps foxes in rural areas need ground shelters or places to hide burrows. Always remember the food chain. Owls eat small mammals. If you want to hear hooting at night, you need to think of hiding and nesting places for these creatures.

Include places where wildlife can give birth and rear their young. Dead trees, old snags, and palms that have recently died attract cavity nesters such as woodpeckers and owls. Do not remove this dead or dying plant material from your yard unless it is located where it may fall on you or your house. Dead fronds on your palms are daytime roosts for mosquito-eating bats.

A source of fresh water, particularly during the winter dry months, attracts wildlife to your landscape. This can be a series of containers such as a birdbath, wet stone for butterflies, or a shallow container full of water buried in the sand for small creatures. One of the most enjoyable features you can create in a backyard wildlife oasis is a small freshwater pond planted with pickerel weed, soft-stem bulrush, and water lilies. Trickling water from a small submerged pump attracts birds. Dragonflies will perch on top of your bulrushes and frogs will miraculously appear and reproduce at will.

As development reduces native habitat, urban and suburban landscapes become more and more important for wildlife survival. Gardening takes on added enjoyment when you are not only using plants to which you are attracted, but also contributing to the survival of our biological heritage.

Ponds

A small pond planted with native aquatic plants and surrounded by a variety of native flowers, shrubs, and small trees is a very nice addition to your landscape. It will be a magnet for a variety of wildlife including birds, butterflies, frogs, and dragonflies and provide you with hours of viewing pleasure.

If you decide to have fish such as koi you will need to do some reading about pumps and filters since waste from the fish must be removed to keep your pond viable. If you don't have a yen for raising fish, other than small mosquito fish that eat mosquito larvae, pond maintenance is very simple with no need for pumps to oxygenate the water or filters to clean out wastes.

Select a site that will have at least a half-day of sunlight if you want to have plants that bloom well. They will thrive in a shady pond but will not bloom as profusely. A pond located in full sun may cause an initial heavy growth of algae until the surface is covered with lilies and other plants, at which time the algae will mostly disappear.

You start your pond by digging a hole in the ground into which you place either a preformed fiberglass shell or a synthetic rubber liner that can be cut to the size of the pond. If you use the preformed fiberglass shell you are clearly constrained in the size and shape of the pond, although the installation will be easier. If you go for the free-form pond, the hole should be two and a half to three feet at its deepest, with sloping sides and a shelf around the edges that is about one foot deep. This will enable you to have a variety of aquatic plants that can grow in different depths of water. You will need to use a pond liner to make your pond watertight. There are several types, including synthetic rubber and polyethylene, and they come in a variety of sizes that can be cut to the size of your pond. As a way of calculating the size of the liner you will need, measure the length and width of the hole and add to each dimension two and a half times the deepest part of the hole and one and a half feet to each side. After the hole is dug, make sure that the edges are level and that the bottom doesn't have any stones or pieces of root that can pierce the liner. If your area is stony, you may want to add an inch or two of sand to the bottom. After you place the liner in the hole and smooth the sides as well as possible, you can cut the edges so they will overlap the sides by about a foot. You can then place rocks and gravel over the edges of the liner or bury them in the surrounding soil.

We have found that plastic oil pans you can buy at an auto supply store provide good containers for planting aquatics in the pond. Place the plant tuber in the pan and fill it with sand. You can place a few fertilizer sticks in the sand to get growth under way. The pan with sand is heavy enough to stay put on the bottom of the pond or on the shelf.

It is not necessary to fertilize the plants subsequently since decaying vegetation will release sufficient nutrients to keep the plants going. Once a year you might wade into the pond to remove any unwanted weeds and debris.

Aquatic plants grow easily and spread rapidly so that a few plants go a long way. They are truly hardy perennials and the only maintenance needed over time will be to divide and thin the plants. In addition to aquatic plants you can also plant some grasses, shrubs, and small trees around the edge to give a hiding place for frogs and resting places for birds.

If you are concerned about mosquitoes, add *Gambusia* minnows that eat mosquito larvae. If you have a pump that circulates water, this will also reduce mosquitoes as they lay eggs in quiet shallow water. Both tadpoles and dragonflies eat mosquito larvae and you can encourage their presence by planting in the pond as well as around it.

Edible Gardening

Your landscape can provide food for both you and the other creatures that inhabit it. You can grow a significant portion of your needed fruits and vegetables in a manner that isn't destructive to the environment. In addition, your homegrown produce will taste better. In fact, once you've eaten fruit that was picked ten minutes earlier rather than waxed and kept in cold storage for months, it will be difficult to return to the grocery store version. In addition, transporting produce from all over the world to our supermarkets is a wasteful, energy-consuming process.

Florida has an ideal climate for growing your own food. In many parts of Florida, tropical as well as deciduous fruit trees will thrive, and with the right combination of varieties, there could be fruit for your table almost year-round. The case for homegrown vegetables is similar. Summer presents some challenges, but spring, fall, and winter are ideal for most traditional "northern garden" vegetables.

For a list of vegetables that can be grown in Florida, with varieties, planting dates in various parts of the state, as well as gardening advice, consult the *Florida Vegetable Gardening Guide* prepared by the Florida Cooperative Extension Service and available online at http://edis.ifas.ufl.edu/VH021. There are a number of tropical vegetables with African, Asian, and Caribbean origins that will thrive in our summer season.

In the case of fruit, there are two climatic aspects that primarily determine whether they will thrive in your part of the state. One is called chilling hours, which are hours below 45°, and the other is freezing temperatures. In order to bear fruit, some fruit trees of temperate origin, such as apples, peaches, and apricots, usually require more chilling hours than occur here except in north Florida, although new low-chilling varieties have been developed that have extended their range southward. On the other hand, many fruits, particularly those of tropical origin, can be badly damaged by freezing temperatures. Listed below are some of the fruits that can be grown in parts of the state designated roughly as north (USDA zones 8A and 8B), central (zones 9A and 9B), and south (zones 10A and 10B). Varieties can differ in their chilling requirements and in their ability to withstand cold weather, so speak to your local cooperative extension agent about varieties of these fruits that do well in your area.

North. Apples, blackberries, blueberries, pears, plums, grapes, figs, nectarines, pecans, peaches, persimmons, oranges (amber sweet variety), mandarins (satsuma variety), kumquats, and strawberries.

Central. Apples, blackberries, blueberries, pears, grapes, figs, nectarines, peaches, persimmons, oranges, grapefruits, kumquats, calamondins, lemons, loquats, strawberries, Persian limes, tangelos, mandarins, tangerines, avocados, bananas, and papayas (sheltered locations).

South. Blackberries, figs, muscadine grapes, oranges, grapefruits, lemons, limes, kumquats, tangelos, mandarins, avocados, papayas, bananas, mangos, pineapples, guavas, tamarinds, loquats, and sapodillas.

You can plant your vegetables in a well-defined kitchen garden or weave them into the landscape along walkways and edges of larger shrubbery. Some will need full sun; others, such as most greens, will thrive best in filtered shade. Many vegetables, although not all, are particular about the months in which they grow. Few of the traditional northern latitude crops will tolerate our hot and humid summers without succumbing to diseases and insects. The gardening season begins here in August or September and extends to the beginning of the rainy season, but the actual planting dates for various crops will depend on which part of Florida you live in.

Composting is an important way for the homeowner to recycle yard and kitchen waste to the vegetable garden. A soil rich in organic matter is needed for the most successful production of vegetables. There are a number of high- and low-tech contraptions and methods for converting kitchen and yard waste into compost that can be incorporated into your soil. There are totally enclosed containers, some of which can be turned and some that are stationary. Compost can be produced from a free-standing open pile on the ground or surrounded by concrete blocks or chicken wire. The piles can be frequently turned over with a pitchfork or allowed to just sit there. Air, water, and a mix of fresh vegetable matter or manure with dry material like straw, hay, leaves, lawn clippings, and newspaper comprise the composting mixture. Almost any organic material will do, but a variety is best. There is a wealth of information on the subject of composting at your local cooperative extension office, on the internet, or in books.

Vegetables and fruits require more feeding and water than the native plants in your landscape. Depending on your soil and the level of its organic material, irrigation and fertilization of some type may be necessary. If you irrigate, use a micro-irrigation system to reduce the amount of water used, and if you fertilize, use a nonsoluble organic fertilizer. If you are fortunate enough to have access to animal manures, apply them after they have aged.

Lawn and noxious weeds near your edibles will grow aggressively into your enriched and well-watered garden spaces and create maintenance problems. You may find it easiest in the long run to create a barrier around your kitchen garden and other edibles. Hefty lumber (not pressure treated), concrete (blocks or poured), borders of mulch, or various other products designed for the task will separate your enriched, food-producing soil from surrounding lawn or plantings. An alternative is container gardening, which works best in small spaces.

Don't use herbicides to get rid of weeds—hand-pick or hoe. Mulch your garden and fruit trees to retain moisture, control weeds, and prevent temperature extremes. As your mulch breaks down it will enrich your soil with organic matter. You can use oil or soap sprays to control some of the garden pests. Remove caterpillars and grasshoppers by hand. Surround your garden with a diversity of native plants to increase niches for beneficial insects that will help control insect pests. Be careful if you do spray since oils and soaps can also kill beneficial insects.

4

Plants and How to Use Them

Trees

Trees are the kings in your landscape. If you do nothing else on your property, plant trees. Trees provide green height and breadth. Trees also provide shade, filter dust from the air, supply oxygen and remove carbon dioxide, shelter urban wildlife, and absorb rainwater. In addition, many studies have shown that they add monetary value to your home as well as value to an entire neighborhood.

No one needs to remind the permanent resident that it is 85° or hotter for four to six months of the year in Florida. Trees perform many beneficial functions, but surely a primary one in this climate is shading. They shade and cool your home, your car, and your street. They also provide a respite from the intense summer sun for many of your smaller plants. Most plants thrive when they are shaded for a portion of the day, particularly from the late afternoon sun.

Trees do many other things. One canopy tree produces a family's supply of oxygen for a year. Trees remove carbon dioxide (the major greenhouse gas), trace metals, and other industrial pollutants such as nitrogen oxide and sulfur dioxide from the air we breathe. The tree canopy intercepts rainwater and slows its fall to the ground during our frequent intense summer storms as well as increasing the absorption of water by the surrounding soil enriched with roots and leaf debris. A 50% canopy can reduce storm water runoff by up to 25%. Storm water runoff carries soil, fertilizers, and other chemicals down storm drains and eventually into our bays and estuaries. This causes algal blooms that cloud these waters and kill sea grasses. Without sea grasses young fish, crustaceans, and other aquatic life have nowhere to feed and hide as they mature. There are inextricable connections between all the elements of the ecosystem. Your landscape is part of it.

Trees provide shelter, food, and homes for urban wildlife. Many migratory bird species fly from the Caribbean islands to the Carolinas, resting and feeding in the pine canopy. Pines also support the large nests of eagles, ospreys, and great horned owls. Seeds from maples, sweet gums, elms, sugarberries, red cedars, and oaks are relished, predictable food sources for our backyard nesting species such as cardinals, northern mockingbirds, and blue jays. Red bay and sweet bay magnolia trees provide larval food for various kinds of swallowtail butterflies.

Plant as many different tree species as the size of your property will allow. Trees come in many different sizes and shapes, from the majestic live oak to small understory trees fifteen to twenty feet tall. In addition to variations in size, trees also differ in their form and the textures and colors of their leaves, flowers, fruit, and bark. Observing these differences can be a source of enjoyment when you become attuned to them. Tables I and II at the end of this section list canopy trees and small trees, respectively. These lists are not exhaustive, but give a broad selection of trees that should be available at native nurseries in your area. Discuss your selections with your local native nursery operator, as well as with other folks in your area who are knowledgeable about them, such as licensed arborists, members of the local native plant society, and master gardeners.

Depending on your location within the state, there are a variety of native trees and shrubs whose flowers and foliage herald spring and autumn seasonal changes, albeit perhaps more subtly than in other parts of the country. You can see more of this diversity close at hand by planting a variety of deciduous trees as well as evergreen trees on your property. We often hear from customers that what they miss most in Florida is the change of seasons. It is certainly true that we don't have the lovely fall leaf color changes, and we don't have many spring flowering trees, at least in the southern two-thirds of the state. If you drive into the countryside in late fall, however, you will see color change in sweet gum leaves in the northern half of the state and in red maple and bald cypress leaves throughout the state. Spring colors include the bright chartreuse greens of new leaves and the various flower colors of our native viburnum, redbud, red maple, plum, and dogwood. Summer brings the blooms of magnolias and bays.

We hear from some people that they don't want to plant deciduous trees because they don't want to rake leaves. They often feel that they have to rake because they want to keep their lawns clear of leaves. If you minimize your lawn as we have suggested and don't establish or maintain turf in the shade of canopy trees, this won't be a problem. Instead you will be blessed with natural mulch for your plantings rather than a nuisance to bag and discard.

We also hear from folks that they are afraid to plant canopy trees because of the damage they might cause in hurricane-force winds. Many native trees have been shown to be relatively wind-resistant, particularly when they are planted in groups. They can actually deflect flying debris, which is a major cause of damage to structures. In order to develop wind resistance they must be well rooted in all directions and expertly pruned throughout their lifetime. Where possible large trees should be planted at least twenty-five feet from structures and impervious surfaces. If this is not possible the trees should be routinely pruned by a certified arborist to shape them properly and limit their growth. Smaller trees (fifteen feet final height) and palms may be planted within ten feet of the house foundation and driveway.

It is tempting to buy the largest trees you can afford with the hope that they will provide shade sooner. Younger trees, however, are less expensive and become established more quickly in your landscape than trees that have been grown under nursery conditions for a longer time. Once planted, they often surpass larger nursery stock within a few years because they experience less stress adapting to existing soil conditions. Also, you do not need to water younger trees as often or for as long. We suggest trees in fifteen-gallon containers as a good compromise. Here in Florida, this size tree can begin to produce significant shade within three to five years. Another strategy would be to buy one large container-grown canopy tree and several smaller canopy trees to create varying heights and maturities in your landscape as you would find in nature. You may want to encourage seedlings on your property if they germinate in advantageous locations and are desirable species. The tree that "plants itself" often grows faster than any container-grown stock.

When planting under large trees, use young shrubs, flowers and ground covers. Trees are often shallowly rooted here due to fluctuations in the water table through the seasons. Smaller plants will be able to adjust more quickly and will not disturb tree roots to the extent that larger specimens will.

Your canopy trees should be native to your region of Florida. This means they will be adapted to local weather and soil conditions. Depending on your locality, they must be cold-hardy or salt-resistant or be able to thrive in wet, low-lying areas. It is expensive and heart-breaking to remove large unsuitable trees, so choose wisely before you plant. Trees are long-lived so that planting one not only affects your property at present, but also can have an impact on you and your neighbors into the future. Plant canopy trees well within the boundaries of your property so that neighbors do not remove limbs that arch out over their lawn. Plant wars between folks who do and do not like trees can be very unpleasant. For this same reason, plant smaller trees in public right of ways or in a sidewalk median or under power lines. If you have a septic system it is best not to plant trees over the drainfield. Plant shallow-rooted shrubs, ground covers, and native clump grasses instead.

Trees can provide a woodland appearance if a variety of species with differing sizes and shapes are used. Walk through a native woodland in your area and you will see that trees grow in clusters often apparently at random, rather than in equally spaced arrays. Understory trees grow beneath the canopy of larger trees as do sabal palms and shrubs. This provides the naturalistic look that we emphasize in this book. It is so important but missing in many new developments. Nothing is as soulless here in Florida as rows of new homes, with new lawns, and a single, centrally placed palm or stick tree. An even sadder sight is an established, older neighborhood of similar barrenness.

Canopy trees increase in value over time and not only beautify your property and neighborhood but define the character of your community. We all say with pleasure "it is a well-treed area." Dr. Thomas Fuller, British physician and historian, wrote in 1732, "He that plants trees loves others besides himself."

Table I. Canopy Trees (taller than 30 feet high at maturity)

Abbreviations

Range: N (north) USDA Zones 8A, 8B, 9A north of Pasco County; C (central) 9A south of Pasco County, 9B; S (south) Zone 10B; SC (south central) 10A

Moisture: Av (average) M (moist) Fl (flooded) D (dry)

Leaves: E (evergreen) De (deciduous) SD (semi-deciduous)

Common Name *Botanical Name*	Range	Av Ht in Feet	Moisture	Leaves	Comment
American Holly *Ilex opaca*	N/C	35	M	E	Handsome evergreen tree with dark green leaves and bright red fruit.

American Sycamore *Platanus occidentalis*	N/C	50	Av/M	De	Fast growth. Needs space. Large distinctive leaves. Mottled bark.
Bald Cypress *Taxodium distichum*	N/C/S	60	Av/Fl	De	Large long-lived tree for wet or average sites. Pest-resistant.
Buttonwood *Conocarpus erectus*	C/S	40	Av/M	E	Green and silver varieties. Good hedge, screen, or specimen for coastal sites and barrier islands.
Coastal Plain Willow *Salix caroliniana*	N/C/S	25–40	M/Fl	De	Fast grower. Attracts butterflies. Tolerant of inundation.
Common Persimmon *Diospyros virginiana*	N/C/S	40–60	Av/D	De	Grows in a wide variety of sites.
Florida Elm *Ulmus americana* var. *floridana*	N/C	50	Av/D/M	De	Fast-growing, handsome, vase-shaped tree.
Gumbo Limbo *Bursera simaruba*	S	50	Av	De	Distinctive peeling copper-colored bark.
Laurel Oak *Quercus laurifolia*	N/C/S	50	Av/Fl	De/SD	Grows in a variety of soil types. Good shade tree. Longevity 60 years.

Common Name *Botanical Name*	Range	Av Ht in Feet	Moisture	Leaves	Comment
Live Oak *Quercus virginiana*	N/C/S	50	Av/D	SD	Needs space. Crown width twice height. Long-lived. Hurricane-resistant.
Loblolly Bay *Gordonia lasianthus*	N/C	35	Av/Fl	E	White fragrant flowers. Prefers semi-shade and undisturbed natural soils.
Loblolly Pine *Pinus taeda*	N/SC	60–80	Av	E	Fast growth. Provides high shade for understory planting.
Longleaf Pine *Pinus palustris*	N/C/S	60	Av/D	E	Long-lived. Good disease resistance. Long bare trunk with small crown.
Magnolia, Southern *Magnolia grandiflora*	N/C	40	Av	E	Large green leaves. Blooms in spring. Several cultivars available.
Magnolia, Sweet Bay *Magnolia virginiana*	N/C	40	M/Fl	E	Small white flowers in spring. Fruit used by wildlife. Butterfly attractor.

Mahogany *Swietenia mahagoni*	S	40	Av/D	E	Distinctive tree for coastal sites. Attractive bark. Long-lived.
Mastic *Sideroxylon foetidissimum*	S	50–70	Av	E	Shade tree. Salt-tolerant. Slow-growing.
Ogeechee Tupelo *Nyssa ogeche*	N/C	50	M	De	Fast-growing. Lovely fall color.
Pigeon Plum *Cocoloba diversifolia*	S	35	Av	E	Fruit attractive to birds. Multicolored peeling bark. Leathery dark green leaves.
Red Cedar, Southern *Juniperus virginiana*	N/C/S	50	D/M	E	Good nesting tree for birds. Can hedge and be used as a living Christmas tree. Salt-tolerant.
Red Bay *Persea borbonia*	N/C/S	40	D/Av	E	Aromatic leaves. Shade tree. Butterfly and bird attractor.
Red Maple *Acer rubrum*	N/C/S	30-50	Av/M	De	Fast-growing shade tree for wet to moist sites. Good spring color.

Abbreviations

Range: N (north) USDA Zones 8A, 8B, 9A north of Pasco County; C (central) 9A south of Pasco County, 9B; S (south) Zone 10B; SC (south central) 10A

Moisture: Av (average) M (moist) Fl (flooded) D (dry)

Leaves: E (evergreen) De (deciduous) SD (semi-deciduous)

Common Name *Botanical Name*	Range	Av Ht in Feet	Moisture	Leaves	Comment
Red Mulberry *Morus rubra*	N/C/S	40–60	M	De	Fast growth. Fruit attracts wildlife. Good shade tree. Fall color.
River Birch *Betula nigra*	N	40–60	M	De	Grows quickly. Shaggy peeling bark. Often planted in clumps.
Shumard Oak *Quercus shumardii*	N/C	50	M/D	De	Fast growth. Good street tree. Good seed producer for wildlife.
Slash Pine *Pinus elliotii*	N/C/S	50	Av/D	E	Fast growth. Nest and food for birds. Light, even shade. Salt-tolerant.
Strangler Fig *Ficus aurea*	C/S	40–60	Av	E	Fast-growing. Large tree for large residential sites. Good shade tree.
Sugarberry *Celtis laevigata*	N/C/S	50	Av/Fl	De	Fast-growing. Good shade tree. Wildlife attractor. Interesting knobby bark.

Sweet Gum *Liquidambar styraciflua*	N/C	50	Av/M	De	Fast-growing. Good shade tree for moist sites. Fall color.
Tulip Tree *Liriodendron tulipifera*	N/C	50–80	M	De	Fast-growing. Handsome single-trunked tree. Attractive flowers. Fall color.
Wild Tamarind *Lysiloma latisiliquum*	S	25–50	Av/D	E	Fast-growing. Attractive bark. Good shade tree. Attractive spring flowers.
Winged Elm *Ulmus alata*	N/C	50	Av/D	De	Corky wings on branches. Nice tree for dry sites. Interesting branch pattern.

Abbreviations

Range: N (north) USDA Zones 8A, 8B, 9A north of Pasco County; C (central) 9A south of Pasco County, 9B; S (south) Zone 10B; SC (south central) 10A

Moisture: Av (average) M (moist) Fl (flooded) D (dry)

Leaves: E (evergreen) De (deciduous) SD (semi-deciduous)

Table II. Small Trees (15 to 30 feet at maturity)

Abbreviations

Range: N (north) USDA Zones 8A, 8B, 9A north of Pasco County; C (central) 9A south
of Pasco County, 9B; S (south) Zone 10B; SC (south central) 10A

Moisture: Av (average) M (moist) Fl (flooded) D (dry)

Leaves: E (evergreen) De (deciduous) SD (semi-deciduous)

Common Name *Botanical Name*	Range	Av Ht in Feet	Moisture	Leaves	Comment
Cherry Laurel *Prunus caroliniana*	N/C	25	Av	E	White fragrant flowers, black fruit. Shiny green lustrous leaves.
Chickasaw Plum *Prunus angustifolia*	N/C	20	D/M	De	White showy fragrant flowers. Black fruit, shiny green leaves.
Chinquapin *Castanea pumila*	N/C	30	D	De	Fall color. Fruit good wildlife food.
Crab Apple *Malus angustifolia*	N/C	15–25	M/D	De	Showy flowers. Fruit attractive to wildlife.
Dahoon Holly *Ilex cassine*	N/C/S	30	Av/Fl	E	Does well in wet soil but can take dryer soils. Red berries for wildlife.
East Palatka Holly *Ilex* x *attenuata* 'East Palatka'	N/C/S	15–25	Av/M	E	Bright red fruit eaten by birds. Leaves dark lustrous green.

Fiddlewood *Citharexylum spinosum*	C/S	20	Av	E	Shrubby small tree. White fragrant flowers. Shiny green leaves.
Flatwoods Plum *Prunus umbellata*	N/C	15	D/M	E	White showy flowers. Fruit a purple drupe.
Flowering Dogwood *Cornus florida*	N/C	30	Av	E	Showy spring flowers. Fruit bright red berry.
Fringe Tree *Chionanthus virginicus*	N/C	25	Av	E	Clusters of creamy spring flowers. Fruit a dark blue drupe.
Geiger Tree *Cordia sebestena*	S	25	Av/D	E	Showy orange-red flowers that can occur anytime during the year.
Jamaica Caper *Capparis cynophallophora*	C/S	15	Av/D	E	Small understory tree for coastal sites. Purplish flowers in spring and summer.
Marlberry *Ardisia escallonioides*	SC/S	10–20	Av/M	E	Coastal in northern range, inland south. Berries attract birds. Shade- and salt-tolerant.

Common Name *Botanical Name*	Range	Av Ht in Feet	Moisture	Leaves	Comment
Myrsine *Rapanea punctata*	C/S	15	Av/M	E	Takes difficult conditions. Salt-tolerant.
Myrtle Oak *Quercis myrtifolia*	N/C/S	30	Av/D	E	Coastal evergreen shrub or small tree.
Pond Apple *Annona glabra*	S	15–30	Av/M	E	Attractive pale yellow flowers. Shiny deep green leaves. Gnarled trunk.
Red Buckeye *Aesculus pavia*	N/C	6–30	M/Av/D	De	Handsome red flowers attract butterflies and humming-birds. Five-part compound leaf.
Redbud *Cercis canadensis*	N/C	15–30	Av	De	Bright magenta flowers before leafing out in spring.
Sand Live Oak *Quercus geminata*	N/C/S	25	D	SD	Conspic-uously turned-under leaves. Good for dry coastal sites.

Abbreviations

Range: N (north) USDA Zones 8A, 8B, 9A north of Pasco County; C (central) 9A south of Pasco County, 9B; S (south) Zone 10B; SC (south central) 10A

Moisture: Av (average) M (moist) Fl (flooded) D (dry)

Leaves: E (evergreen) De (deciduous) SD (semi-deciduous)

Satin Leaf *Chrysophyllum oliviforme*	S	25	Av	E	Reddish-brown bark. Upper leaf dark green, lower copper-colored.
Sea Grape *Coccoloba uvifera*	C/S	15–20	Av/D	E	Coastal plant. Large orbicular leaves green with reddish veins.
Simpson's Stopper *Myrcianthes fragrans*	C/S	15–20	Av	E	Aromatic leaves, fragrant white flowers, reddish peeling bark.
Spicewood *Calyptranthes pallens*	S	20	Av/M	E	Fragrant foliage. Lustrous leaves. Attractive to birds.
Sweet Acacia *Acacia farnesiana*	C/S	8–20	Av/D	SD	Yellow fragrant flowers. Thorny, salt- and drought-tolerant.
Walter's Viburnum *Viburnum obovatum*	N/C/S	25	Av/M	SD	Covered with small white flowers in spring. Fruit black berry. Hedges well.
Wild Lime *Zanthoxylum fagara*	C/S	25	Av/D	E	Small shrubby tree with thorns. Good butterfly attractor.
Witch Hazel *Hamamelis virginiana*	N	20	Av/M	De	Yellow flowers in fall.

Shrubs

If trees are the kings of your landscape, shrubs are the workhorses. They add lasting color and texture to the middle layer of your landscape. They are the most important sources of seeds, berries, and shelter for wildlife living on your property. They can provide a visual buffer between your property and your neighbors, and between your property and the street. Traditionally, shrubs have been used as foundation plantings or as hedges. We suggest that shrubs be spread randomly among your trees, giving a naturalistic look to your landscape. Select a few different species of shrubs that do well in your area and plant them repeatedly.

Shrubs are multi-trunked woody plants varying in height from two feet to twenty feet. They vary in leaf texture and shape from compact and small-leaved plants such as viburnums to large leaved plants such as fiddlewood and oakleaf hydrangea. Leaf color also varies from the red of firebush, the yellow green of wax myrtle to the dark green of yaupon holly. Fruits of hollies are bright red, American beautyberry has white or purple fruit, while firebush, wild coffee, and Florida privet have blue-black fruit. Sea grape, cocoplum, and elderberry have edible fruit. You can derive great pleasure by attuning yourself to the subtle differences that native shrubs provide to your landscape. You can enjoy them whether looking out through your windows or sitting amongst them. We think you will find that, with the varieties of leaf colors and textures that shrubs provide, you won't need dramatic floral displays.

If you don't have the space for a tree, you can use some of the larger shrubs as substitutes. In a small yard, two or three large shrubs will provide the leaf mass and shade of a small tree. Remove the lowest branches and underplant them with small shrubs, grasses, and ferns to create a naturalistic setting. Tall shrubs are an excellent substitute for trees under power lines or in constricted spaces such as between a sidewalk and the street.

Choose large shrubs carefully (six to fifteen feet; see Table III). Final size is a major consideration. Make sure you know how large the shrub will become and plant it where it can grow with no or minimal trimming.

This is especially true under windows and in the front yard. Plant a tall shrub no closer than twelve feet from the foundation. Constant pruning, as well as over fertilizing and watering, can encourage infestations of leaf-sucking insects that prefer tender new foliage. Mechanical or insect wounding of the leaves and stems may result in the introduction of fungal and viral diseases.

Don't use large shrubs as a "green" fence similar to a wooden fence, or a stone/concrete wall. If your space is limited and your primary goal is to screen the sides of your property, it is probably better to install a wooden fence or lattice and then plant smaller shrubs and vines in front of it. A wood fence or lattice creates instant privacy, but it will take three to four years for a single row of shrubs to do likewise. In addition, it will require a considerable amount of pruning to restrict the lateral and vertical growth of the shrubs. If individual shrubs die, the replacement shrubs will require a number of years to fill in the gap. Shady borders are particularly problematic since shrubs will not grow thickly under trees or where they will be shaded by your home.

If you have at least an eight-foot depth along any of your borders, you can screen your property by planting multiple species of small trees and shrubs that will provide contrasting textures, colors, and berries for wildlife. If you have a depth of twelve to twenty-plus feet, we think it is more interesting to plant a variety of trees and shrubs of varying heights that are several plants deep, but not in rows. Nature abhors a straight line and even spacing. This approach enables you to block views without creating an impenetrable fortress look. The result is a beautiful buffer seen from either your house or from the street. It will be exciting to look at through the seasons as birds and butterflies and other wildlife move in and out to feed on berries and/or nectar. It will create a far more interesting view than an asphalted street, parked and passing cars, your neighbor's driveway, or worse—the interior of your neighbor's living room.

Table III. Large Shrubs (4–30 feet)

Abbreviations

Range: N (north) USDA Zones 8A, 8B, 9A north of Pasco County; C (central) 9A
    south of Pasco County, 9B; S (south) Zone 10B; SC (south central) 10A
Moisture: Av (average) M (moist) Fl (flooded) D (dry)
Leaves: E (evergreen) De (deciduous) SD (semi-deciduous)

Common Name *Botanical Name*	Range	Av Ht in Feet	Moisture	Leaves	Comment
Adam's Needle *Yucca filamentosa*	N/C	4–10	D	E	Salt-tolerant. Adaptable. Showy white flowers. Low basal leaves.
Arrowwood *Viburnum dentatum*	N/C	6–15	M	De	Showy white flowers. Blue fruit that attracts wildlife.
Bahama Senna *Senna mexicana* var. *chapmanii*	N/C	6	Av	E	Golden yellow flowers blooms much of the year. Butterfly attractor.
Beautyberry *Callicarpa americana*	N/C/S	6	Av/D	De	Birds attracted to red or white berries, bees to pink flowers. Part sun or shade.
Buttonbush *Cephalanthus occidentalis*	N/C/S	10	M/Fl	De	Fragrant flowers attract butterflies and bees. Good in disturbed soils.
Cherokee Bean *Erythrina herbacea*	N/C/S	6–15	Av/D	De	Spikes of red flowers in spring before leaves. Red seeds. Spiny.

Christmas Berry *Lycium carolinianum*	N/C/S	3–9	M	E	Blue flowers, red berries. Highly salt-tolerant.
Cocoplum *Chrysobalanus icaco*	S/C	15	Av	E	Excellent wildlife attractor. Upright form is salt-tolerant, red-tipped is not.
Fiddlewood *Citharexylum spinosum*	S/SC	18	D/Av	E	Attractive foliage. Good for wildlife. Salt- and drought-tolerant.
Firebush *Hamelia patens*	S/SC	4–10	Av/D	E	Flowers and fruit attract wildlife. Leaf color in shade, flowers in sun.
Florida Azalea *Rhododendron austrinum*	N	4–8	M	De	Showy fragrant orange flowers.
Florida Privet *Forestiera segregata*	N/C/S	6–15	D/Av/M	SD	Berries good wildlife food. Drought- and salt-tolerant. Tolerates pruning.
Marlberry *Ardisia escallonioides*	S/SC	6–12	Av/M	E	White fragrant flowers. Fruit attract birds. Shade- and salt-tolerant.

Abbreviations

Range: N (north) USDA Zones 8A, 8B, 9A north of Pasco County; C (central) 9A south of Pasco County, 9B; S (south) Zone 10B; SC (south central) 10A

Moisture: Av (average) M (moist) Fl (flooded) D (dry)

Leaves: E (evergreen) De (deciduous) SD (semi-deciduous)

Common Name *Botanical Name*	Range	Av Ht in Feet	Moisture	Leaves	Comment
Myrsine *Rapanea punctata*	C/S	8–15	D/M	E	Good hedge plant. Takes difficult conditions. Salt-tolerant.
Necklace Pod *Sophora tomentosa*	C/S	6–10	Av	E	Yellow flowers attract wildlife. Drought- and salt-tolerant.
Oakleaf Hydrangea *Hydrangea quercifolia*	N/C	4–8	Av/D	De	Showy white flowers. Fall color. Exfoliating bark.
Pinxter Azalea *Rhododendron canescens*	N/C	10–15	Av/M	De	Showy pinkish fragrant flowers.
Pipestem *Agarista populifolia*	N/C	6–14	M/D	E	Shade only. Clusters of aromatic bell-like flowers. Easy to grow.
Red Buckeye *Aesculus pavia*	N/C	6–30	Av/M	De	Red flowers attract wildlife. Good understory shrub.
Sea Grape *Coccoloba uvifera*	SC/S	10–20	Av/D	E	Extremely salt-tolerant. Fruit good for wildlife. Gives tropical look.
Scarlet Hibiscus *Hibiscus coccineus*	N/C	4–6	M/Fl	De	Large red flowers. Fast grower. Dies back after frost but returns.

Simpson's Stopper *Myrcianthes fragrans*	N/C/S	5–20	Av	E	Fragrant flowers and leaves. Berries attract birds. Attractive peeling bark
Snowbell *Styrax americanus*	N/C	6–10	M/Fl	De	Moist, shady sites. Flowers profusely.
Sparkleberry *Vaccinium arboreum*	N/C	6–20	Av/M	De	White flowers. Berries for wildlife. Reddish bark. Does well in shade.
Spanish Stopper *Eugenia foetida*	S	10–20	Av	E	Fruit attractive to birds. Good for narrow spaces.
Strawberry Bush *Euonymus americanus*	N/C	10–15	M	De	Shade lover with strawberry-like fruit. Multi-stemmed, green bark.
Summersweet *Clethra alnifolia*	N/C	3–10	Av/M	De	Fragrant white flowers attract butterflies. Fall color. Shade-tolerant.
Sweet Shrub *Calycanthus floridus*	N	6–10	M	De	Red fragrant flowers, yellow autumn leaves. Good for shaded areas.

Abbreviations

Range: N (north) USDA Zones 8A, 8B, 9A north of Pasco County; C (central) 9A south of Pasco County, 9B; S (south) Zone 10B; SC (south central) 10A

Moisture: Av (average) M (moist) Fl (flooded) D (dry)

Leaves: E (evergreen) De (deciduous) SD (semi-deciduous)

Common Name *Botanical Name*	Range	Av Ht in Feet	Moisture	Leaves	Comment
Titi *Cyrilla recemiflora*	N/C	10–25	Av/M	E	Profuse spring bloomer, white racemes. Attracts bees. Thicket-forming.
Virginia Willow *Itea virginica*	C/N/S	4–8	Av/Fl	De	Showy spring flower clusters, fall color. Good shrub for wet areas.
Walter's Viburnum *Viburnum obovatum*	N/C/S	10–20	Av/M	SD	White spring flowers. Fruit for wildlife. Can be hedged.
Wax Myrtle *Myrica cerifera*	N/C/S	6–20	D/M	E	Provides food and cover for wildlife. Tough, salt-tolerant. Fast-growing.
Wild Coffee *Pyschotria nervosa*	C/S	5–10	Av/M	E	Glossy green leaves with attractive venation. Good for shade. Wildlife attractor.
Wild Sage *Lantana involucrata*	SC/S	4	Av/D	E	Butterflies attracted to flower clusters. Drought-tolerant.
Yaupon Holly *Ilex vomitoria*	N/C/S	10–20	D/Av/M	E	Red berries good wildlife food. Salt-tolerant. Many cultivars.

Yellow Anise *Illicium parviflorum*	N/C	6–20	Av/M	E	Dark green aromatic leathery leaves. Shade-tolerant.

Table IV. Small Shrubs (<4 feet)

Abbreviations

Range: N (north) USDA Zones 8A, 8B, 9A north of Pasco County; C (central) 9A south of Pasco County, 9B; S (south) Zone 10B; SC (south central) 10A

Moisture: Av (average) M (moist) Fl (flooded) D (dry)

Leaves: E (evergreen) De (deciduous) SD (semi-deciduous)

Common Name *Botanical Name*	Range	Av Ht in Feet	Moisture	Leaves	Comment
Cocoplum *Chrysobalanus icaco* cv 'Horizontal'	C/S	1–2	D	E	Salt-tolerant.
Coontie *Zamia pumila*	N/C/S	2–3	Av/D	E	Best planted in a mass. Cold-, drought-, and salt-tolerant. Full sun to part shade.
Dwarf Walter's Viburnum *Viburnum obovatum*	N/C/S	2–3	E	E	The cultivar Mrs. Schiller's Delight blooms seven months of the year.
Dwarf Yaupon Holly *Ilex vomitoria*	N/C/S	2–3	D/Av/M	E	Same as for Yaupon but dwarfed.
Golden Creeper *Ernodea littoralis*	C/S	1–2	D	E	Salt-tolerant dune and beach plant. Forms mats.

Common Name *Botanical Name*	Range	Av Ht in Feet	Moisture	Leaves	Comment
Inkberry *Scaevola plumieri*	C/S	2–5	D	E	Salt-tolerant coastal plant. White to pink flowers.
Sea Oxeye *Borrichia frutescens*	N/C/S	5	M	E	Colony-forming perennial. Good for wet coastal saline conditions. Yellow daisylike flower.
Seaside Elder *Iva imbricata*	N/C	2–5	D	E	Sun- and salt-tolerant. Forms colonies from underground stems.

Abbreviations

Range: N (north) USDA Zones 8A, 8B, 9A north of Pasco County; C (central) 9A south of Pasco County, 9B; S (south) Zone 10B; SC (south central) 10A

Moisture: Av (average) M (moist) Fl (flooded) D (dry)

Leaves: E (evergreen) De (deciduous) SD (semi-deciduous)

Ground covers

We believe that the most important function of ground covers is to replace turf. There are two approaches to doing this. The traditional way is to define ground covers as perennial plants that "hug" the ground and spread quickly by underground rhizomes or by rooting at each node. By this definition the best ground covers are those that so thoroughly cover the ground that weeds are effectively excluded. They are green all year, and not so invasive that it is difficult to contain them in the desired area.

One of the few natives that approximates these requirements is sunshine mimosa—although it can be hard to control. Mimosa, which is native to north and central Florida, has attractive feathery foliage and numerous pink blooms. Mimosa covers the ground quickly and works well in situations where it can be mowed to remove spent blooms and keep weeds from coming through. It will burn after frosty nights but recovers, although it looks sparser in cold weather because the leaflets close up. Mimosa can be useful in open areas where a green ground cover is desired, and unlike grass it doesn't require watering, fertilizing, or treatment for pests.

Sea purslane is a plant that could also be used as a ground cover, particularly along beachfronts where weeds may not be problematic, since it is unlikely that it can be mowed. Unlike the wispy character of mimosa, sea purslane has fleshy leaves. It has attractive flowers, is salt-tolerant, and can thrive in either moist or dry sites.

The native prostrate porterweed is another possible ground cover in south and south central Florida. It grows thickly, but like sea purslane cannot be mowed. It attracts butterflies and has a long blooming season.

Table V describes some other low-growing plants, including vines, which can be considered ground covers. None of them is able to cover the ground quickly enough to exclude weeds and they are not mowable. They can, however, function as ground covers over small areas, particularly if they are mulched well.

An alternative way to think about ground covers, however, is to consider any vegetation as ground cover if it can be used to replace lawn. From an aesthetic standpoint, why substitute one low-growing plant material for another? Large expanses of this kind of ground cover can be just as sterile-looking as large expanses of lawn. We believe it is more visually appealing and naturalistic to plant trees, shrubs, ferns, and native clump grasses and mulch around them. Using a greater diversity of plant materials will also attract more wildlife, one of the major goals of naturalistic planting.

Table V. Ground covers

Abbreviations: N (north) C (central) S (south) SC (south central) Av (average) D (dry) M (moist) S (sun) PSh (partial shade)

Common Name *Botanical Name*	Range	Ht (ft)	Moisture	Sun	Comments
Beach Dune Sunflower *Helianthus debilis*	SC/S	1–2	D/Av	S/PSh	Bright yellow flowers. Grows well in sand, takes other dry sites. Reseeding annual.
Coral Honeysuckle *Lonicera sempervirens*	N/C/S	1–2	Av	S/PSh	Vining plant that can be used as a ground cover. Red tubular flowers attract butterflies, hummingbirds.
Golden Creeper *Ernodea littoralis*	C/S	1–2	D	S/PSh	Salt-tolerant dune and beach plant. Forms mats.
Gopher Apple *Licania michauxii*	N/C/S	1	D	S	Spreads in poor dry sandy soils. Very hardy and slow-growing.
Prostrate Porterweed *Stachytarpheta jamaicensis*	C/S	1–2	Av	S	Blue flowers much of the year. Attracts butterflies.
Railroad Vine *Ipomoea pes-caprae*	N/C/S	0.5	D	S	Showy lavender flowers. Spreads rapidly. Very drought- and salt-tolerant.

Sea Purslane *Sesuvium portulacastrum*	N/C/S	0.5–1	M/D	S	Perennial evergreen. Mat-forming. Pink flowers year around. Salt-tolerant.
Sunshine mimosa *Mimosa strigillosa*	N/C/SC	0.5	D/Av/M	S	Showy pink flower heads. Grows rapidly into a dense mat. Finely divided leaves.
Wild Plumbago *Plumbago scandens*	C/S	1.5	Av	S/PSh	Hardy coastal plant flowers much of the year. Good for butterflies.
Yellow Jessamine *Gelsemium sempervirens*	N/C/S	1	Av/M	S/PSh	Yellow flowers early spring. Good vine as well as ground cover.

Palms

Plant canopy trees before anything else in your landscape. Next, think of planting native palms as they are the signature plants in much of Florida. For a truly tropical look, plant palms around and under your major canopy trees. Use large trees to provide shade, but plant palms if you have a small property or some small spaces where trees won't fit or a beachfront property where trees do not thrive. Palms differ structurally from trees such as oaks and pines. They are grasslike with smaller fibrous root systems. As a consequence, you can plant most palms where space is at a premium, although the royal palm is an exception.

Of the approximately 2,700 species of palms recognized in the world, twelve are native to Florida. These twelve palms vary in size and shape as well as their ability to tolerate various conditions such as cold, salt, sun, and shade.

Some are treelike, either large or small, while others can be used like shrubs.

The sabal palm, the state tree of both Florida and South Carolina, is easy to grow, is hardy, long-lived, and resistant to drought and salt. In addition, it is exceptionally resistant to hurricanes and is the most commonly planted palm in Florida. This palm should be planted in clusters and will produce shade under these conditions. Unlike canopy trees, the sabal palm can be planted within eight to ten feet of your house and can be used to frame entranceways and other architecturally interesting features of your house.

Birds drop sabal palm seeds—if that happens, you will have sabal palm seedlings germinating in your landscape if you don't mow. They will make an attractive shrublike plant during the eight to ten years needed to produce a clear trunk. If you don't want lots of sabal palms, pull out the seedlings while they are still small, as they will be almost impossible to remove when they become larger. The stem bases of the sabal palm, known as boots, remain on some individual palms, while on others they drop off. Those that remain can become growing places for various plants such as bromeliads and ferns as well as some insects. If you buy palms with a trunk you can choose between the two types.

The paurotis palm, although treelike in height, is a natural clump-forming palm with dense foliage. This palm is adaptable to many growing conditions from shade to full sun and well-drained to swampy soils. It is also tolerant of salt. The royal palm is a large tree, up to 100 feet in height—too large for most landscapes. It is mostly used as a street tree and also planted around some commercial buildings.

Some native palms can be useful as shrubs such as saw palmetto, blue-stem palmetto, and needle palm. Both blue-stem palmetto and needle palm are understory plants and can tolerate a considerable amount of shade. Saw palmetto can take full sun to full shade, tolerates dry to wet sites, and is salt-tolerant. There is an attractive native variant of the saw palmetto that has bluish-gray fronds and grows more rapidly than the usual green variety.

Brittle thatch palm and silver palm make attractive small trees in coastal areas in the southern area of the state and are tolerant of salt and dry conditions.

A characteristic of all of these native palms is that they tend to be tough and long-lived. They also have the advantage of being relatively hurricane-resistant. They are slow growing and require no pruning. Never remove the green fronds unless there is an access problem. The stalks with flowers and fruit are essential high-nutrition wildlife foods and should not be removed unless absolutely necessary. Don't plant palms where dropped berries will be a problem. Do not remove yellowing or dead-appearing fronds from the palms, but allow them to drop naturally. Premature frond removal will cause loss of nutrients and shorten the life of the palm.

Native palms can thrive without fertilization or added water, unlike exotic palms that require fertilization three or four times a year to remain healthy.

Table VI. Palms

Abbreviations: N (north) C (central) S (south) SC (south central) Av (average) D (dry) M (moist) Ht (height) ft (feet)

Common Name *Botanical Name*	Range	Av Ht (ft)	Moisture	Comments
Brittle Thatch Palm *Thrinax morrisii*	S	6–15	Av/D	Tolerates wind, salt, drought, and light frost. Best in full sun along the coast.
Sabal Palm *Sabal palmetto*	N/C/S	40	Av/M	Wide adaptability. Tough and sturdy. Plant in clusters. Wildlife eat fruit. Crown good for nesting birds.
Blue-Stem Palmetto *Sabal minor*	N/C/S	8	Av/M	Good for difficult areas. Adaptable to a variety of soils. Fruit attracts wildlife. Good understory shrub.

Common Name *Botanical Name*	Range	Av Ht (ft)	Moisture	Comments
Needle Palm *Rhapidophyllum hystrix*	N/C	3–8	M	Slow-growing, long-lived. Trunk covered with spines. Can grow in shade. Clump former.
Paurotis Palm *Acoelorrhaphe wrightii*	C/S	20–30	Av/M	Clump-forming multi-stemmed palm. Dense foliage. Slow-growing, salt-tolerant. Grows in shade but tolerates sun if kept moist.
Royal Palm *Roystonea regia*	SC/S	60–100	M	Adaptable to street-side planting. Requires full sun. Long-lived. Majestic.
Saw Palmetto *Serenoa repens*	N/C/S	3–20	D/Av/M	Long-lived usually prostrate clump palm. Fruit attractive to wildlife. Tolerates difficult conditions. Silver cultivar available.
Scrub Palmetto *Sabal etonia*	C/S	4–6	D	Takes heat, drought, sun. Long-lived. Good as a small shrub in sandy well-drained conditions.
Silver Palm *Coccothrinax argentata*	C/S	5–15	D	Attractive small tree that tolerates wind, drought, salt spray, and light freezes. Dark green leaf surface, silvery below.

Abbreviations: N (north) C (central) S (south) SC (south central) Av (average) D (dry) M (moist) Ht (height) ft (feet)

Vines

One of the first things new homeowners often do is remove vines from their "overgrown" yards. They do this so that vine-laden trees and shrubs will not be smothered and will receive more sunlight and air circulation. Though it is true that vines can become too rampant in urban/suburban landscapes, it is also important to realize, before you pull them all down and out of your vegetation, that native vines have important roles in nature. Vines that have evolved over time with our local native trees and shrubs are not, generally speaking, as invasive as many of the exotic vines that grow up and out of your yard with the potential to consume the neighborhood. A few examples of the latter are red passion vine, potato vine, and skunk vine. Exotic vines are often showy but uncontrollable. They are not always attractive to wildlife or subject to insect predation and thus natural controls. Don't plant invasive exotic vines and do remove those present in your landscape.

Native vines can play a variety of useful roles in your landscape. Their dense intertwining foliage hides bird nests from snakes, other predatory birds, and domestic cats. Some have thorns, which are a further deterrent to predators. Dense foliage also provides protection from winter storms. Their flowers provide significant amounts of nectar for local butterflies, birds, and insect pollinators. Many produce large quantities of fruit in the fall and thus provide a reliable food source for migratory birds as well as year-round wildlife.

Native vines can easily be controlled by tracing back vining stem growth to the ground and then cutting them off at the base. The upper vine will starve and die off and deteriorate and the wind will blow the leaves out of your trees and shrubs. This should be done every two to three years if the vines overtake the native vegetation. Cutting vines back takes the place of local fires caused by lightening storms that would have limited their potential in nature.

Vines can play other roles in the landscape. They can be planted at the base of four-by-eight-foot trellises to quickly shade walls. On trellised walls at the edge of your property line they will provide privacy between you and your neighbors. This is especially important in narrow side yards where there is not enough space for larger shrubs or trees. Trellised in the back yard, they will similarly camouflage views of neighboring pool cages, sheds, and playground equipment. An obvious use is to let them twine through chain-link fencing to soften its look or climb up and over long expanses of wood fencing, creating a beautiful floral wall. While it may be necessary to do some trimming, vines used in these situations are fast-growing problem solvers.

It is not necessary to trellis vines. Plant them at the base of trees and shrubs to create a more naturalistic setting. Use them as ground covers and let them flow over themselves. Ground vines work especially well with clump grasses and wildflowers in both sunny and shady areas in place of turf.

Intermix two or three species by planting them together or close to each other. Differences in textures, colors, flowering periods, etc., will provide added interest and attract different types of butterflies and other pollinators. Table VII shows a representative list of available native vines.

Table VII. Vines

Abbreviations: N (north) C (central) S (south) S (sun) Sh (shade) PSh (part shade) Av (average) M (moist) D (dry) De (deciduous) E (evergreen) SD (semi-deciduous)

Common Name *Botanical Name*	Range	Light	Moisture	Leaves	Comment
Climbing Hydrangea *Decumaria barbara*	N/C	Sh	M	De	White fragrant flowers. Shiny dark green leaves.
Coral honeysuckle *Lonicera sempervirens*	N/C	S/PSh	Av/M	E	Red flowers attract hummingbirds. Trellises well or as ground cover.
Corky Stem Passion Flower *Passiflora suberosa*	C/S	S/PSh	Av/D	E	Small yellow-green flowers. Attracts butterflies.
Cross Vine *Bignonia capreolata*	N/C	S/Sh	D/Av/M	E	Red/yellow showy trumpet-like flowers in spring.
Jacquemontia *Jacquemontia pentatha*	C/S	S	Av/D	E	Fast-growing, delicate blue flowers. Trellises well.
Muscadine Grape *Vitus rotundifolia*	N/C	S	Av	De	Edible fruit. Grows on trellis or fence.
Passion Flower *Passiflora incarnata*	C/S	S/PSh	Av	E	Purple flowers. Edible fruit. Butterfly attractor.

Common Name *Botanical Name*	Range	Light	Moisture	Leaves	Comment
Trumpet Creeper *Campsis radicans*	N/C/S	S/PSh	Av	De	Flowers showy, tubular orange to red spring and summer.
Wild Allamanda *Urechites lutea*	SC/S	S/PSh	Av	E	Showy yellow flowers. Coastal sites in central Florida.
Yellow Jessamine *Gelsemium sempervirens*	N/C/S	S/PSh	Av/M	E	Yellow flowers early spring. Also can be used as a ground cover.

Abbreviations: N (north) C (central) S (south) S (sun) Sh (shade) PSh (part shade) Av (average) M (moist) D (dry) De (deciduous) E (evergreen) SD (semi-deciduous)

Grasses

Native grasses grow naturally at the beach, in wetlands, pine prairies, and woodlands. They are not turf or lawn grasses that are invasive, exotic, and hungry and thirsty consumers of various resources. Native grasses don't require fertilization, irrigation, or pest control. We feel that they are underutilized in landscapes.

Grasses can be either clump-forming or rhizome-forming. The clump-forming grasses will grow naturally in mounds or clumps. They mix well with wildflowers and other perennials and will not become invasive. The width of the clumps will increase slowly with time. The rhizome-forming grasses behave more like turf grasses and spread by underground stems or rhizomes. They spread rapidly, can become invasive, and are most useful for holding soil in place. On beaches they stabilize drifting sands and withstand hurricane-force winds, while inland they can be planted on banks to minimize erosion. They are used to naturalize the edges of retention ponds.

Most native grasses used in landscapes are clump grasses. Some native clump grasses, such as gamma grass, may grow six to eight feet tall. Others, such as the love grasses, grow only about eighteen inches tall. Some have bluish leaf blades, others are deep emerald green. In the fall and winter many become golden in color and develop beautiful seed heads that are not only decorative but cherished by birds and other wildlife.

Used in clusters, native clump grasses add a soft, breezy feel to a planting because they are not rigid in structure and are not woody like shrubs and trees. They work well when used in mass plantings with wildflowers as they create a pastoral appearance that you will never have to mow.

Besides all of the above features they are also very hardy, long-lasting, and easily grown. Insects don't consume them, they don't have to be trimmed, and they don't get moldy if they are spaced properly so that air circulates around and through them. Some folks trim off the brown stems at the end of the growing season. This is not necessary, but if you do trim wait until winter is almost over. It may be desirable to separate bunch grass tufts every three or four years if the center of the clump has died out. Again, wait until the end of winter then cut the stems almost to the ground. Dig up the bunch, divide it with a shovel or saw, and replant the individual pieces.

Table VIII. Native Grasses

Abbreviations: N (north) C (central) S (south) S (sun) Sh (shade) PSh (part shade) Av (average) M (moist) D (dry)

Common Name *Botanical Name*	Range	Ht(feet)	Moisture	Comments
Eastern Gamma Grass *Tripsacum dactyloides*	N/C/S	4–8	M	Tolerates various soils. Good for slope stabilization. Grows thickly. Reseeding bunch grass. For shade or sun.
Elliott's Love Grass *Eragrostis elliottii*	N/C/S	1–3	D/Av/M	Attractive leaves and flowers. Grows well in dry sandy soils. Good in mass or borders. Reseeding bunch grass.
Florida Gamma Grass *Tripsacum floridanum*	C/S	2–3	Av	Shorter and finer-leaved than Eastern Gamagrass. Bunch grass.
Maidencane *Panicum hemitomon*	N/C/S	1–5	M	Fast-growing, spreads rapidly. Useful for wet areas. Can be difficult to maintain.
Muhly Grass *Muhlenbergia capillaris*	N/C/S	2–4	Av	Showy pink flowers in late fall. Can grow in dry sandy soil. Bunch grass.
Purple Love Grass *Eragrostis spectabilis*	N/C/S	1–3	D/Av/M	Flower panicles with a purplish cast. Grows well in dry sandy soils. Handsome bunch grass.
Salt Meadow Cordgrass *Spartina patens*	N/C/S	2–3	M/Fl	Grows fast. Useful as a ground cover under moist saline or fresh water conditions. Rhizome-forming.

Sand Cordgrass *Spartina bakeri*	N/C/S	3–5	Av/M	Robust bunch grass able to handle a variety of soil moisture conditions. Tolerates salt.
Sea Oats *Uniola paniculata*	N/C/S	3–5	D	Beach-stabilizing grass. Tolerates salt, wind, and dry sandy soil. Rhizome-forming.
Seaside Paspalum *Paspalum vaginatum*	N/C/S	2–3	M	Salt-tolerant, mat-forming, prefers wet sandy soil. Good for stabilization.
Upland River Oats *Chasmanthium latifolium*	N/C	2	Av/D	Similar appearance to sea oats but prefers shade. Will colonize.

Wildflowers

Native annual wildflowers germinate, grow, flower, seed, and die in one season. In north and north central Florida, and in most other parts of the country, the growing season is ended with a killing frost. In south central and south Florida, *season* is more ambiguous since there are years in which there is no killing frost so that some annuals can live for more than one year.

Our common native annual wildflowers produce profuse amounts of seed that germinate and give you masses of blooms year after year, unlike non-native annuals that have been manipulated horticulturally so they do not produce viable seed. Beach dune sunflower (*Helianthus debilis*), Indian blanket (*Gaillardia pulchella*), tropical sage (*Salvia coccinea*), coreopsis (*Coreopsis* spp.), and black-eyed susan (*Rudbeckia hirta*) are five of the easiest wildflowers to grow in sunny spots in your yard.

You may know beach dune sunflower from seeing it growing amongst sea oats on our shifting beach sands. Indian blanket grows just shoreside of the dunes in dry, sandy, shelly environs. Both of these plants will obviously thrive in dry, sunny, harsh spots in your yard. Plant and water them several times and then let them go. Too much mulch, water, or fertilizer kills these hardy wildflowers. Tropical sage (red salvia) prefers some shade, at least for a few hours in the afternoon. It prefers soils with a little organic matter, mulch, and occasional watering to grow lushly in your yard. The two species of coreopsis commonly available in Florida are *C. floridana* (Florida tickseed) and *C. leavenworthii* (tickseed). Both tickseeds are wetland edge ditch plants that seed prolifically if planted in wet places. Even once-a-week irrigation in dry landscapes is sufficient. Plant coreopsis at the base of your air-conditioner unit where water drips onto the ground and you will be rewarded with bright, small, yellow blooms most of the year.

The best part about growing these annuals is that before dying they produce seed, and then seedlings germinate at the base of the parent plant or wherever birds, wind, or rain may have carried the seed. You plant the first wildflowers and then biology takes over and naturalizes your landscape. Each year there are new surprises because your well-thought-out planting spot may not be where new plants germinate next spring (February/March) or even next month. If you are unhappy with plants that grow where you didn't plant them, don't plant reseeding annuals. If you delight in discovering new plants wherever they germinate, these easily grown reseeding wildflowers are for you.

You can prolong the life of these annuals by removing spent blooms, but don't try to encourage new life by constantly watering and fertilizing the original plant. Once it has seeded and become weak, woody, or unsightly, remove it. Let seedlings germinate in the newly exposed bare or lightly mulched ground.

Most perennial flowers, defined as plants that live two or more years, do not live as long here as they do in other areas of the country. You will be lucky if your non-native perennial plants last more than one or two seasons, although there are exceptions such as the non-native pentas, which can last for three or four seasons. Books on perennials list many plants that are supposed to do well in the growing zones 8, 9, and 10 that we have here in Florida. Many of these perennials will do well if you are in those zones in California and even in Texas. Those states do not have our hot, wet summers, which cause most of these perennials to do poorly in Florida. There are non-native plants being sold now as "Florida-friendly." Some of these plants seem to be able to survive in our difficult climate. You will need to try them to determine whether they do well under the conditions in your yard.

Our native perennials, which have evolved in this climate, are better able to take the summers and can last for a number of years. The table below describes some of the native perennials that may have a longer lifespan here, but even some of them can be quite finicky with regard to soil conditions. Those plants that increase their clump size via underground structures, such as yellow canna lily, blue-flag iris and string lily, are more likely to have an extended life. In the end, though, you will also have to try these native perennials to see how long they live in your yard.

Table IX. Wildflowers

Abbreviations: N (north) C (central) S (south) S (sun) Sh (shade) PSh (part shade) Av (average) M (moist) D (dry)

Common Name *Botanical Name*	Range	Moisture	Light	Comments
Beach Dune Sunflower *Helianthus debilis*	SC/S	Av/D	S/PSh	Bright yellow flowers. Grows well in sand but can take other dry sites. Salt-tolerant. Reseeding annual.

Common Name *Botanical Name*	Range	Moisture	Light	Comments
Black-eyed Susan *Rudbeckia hirta*	N/C/S	Av	S/PSh	Copiously reseeding short-lived perennial. Yellow ray flowers, brownish disk flowers.
Blanket Flower *Gaillardia pulchella*	N/C/S	D	S	Copiously reseeding annual. Brightly colored yellow-tipped red rays. Can't take moist soil.
Blue-flag Iris *Iris virginica*	N/C	Av/M	S/PSh	Showy blue spring to summer flowers. Good for edges of water bodies. Spreads. Perennial.
Butterfly Weed *Asclepias tuberosa*	N/C/S	Av/D	S	Long-lived reseeding perennial. Orange flowers in showy clusters. Intolerant of wet or disturbed soils.
Cardinal Flower *Lobelia cardinalis*	N/C	M	S/PSh	Attractive scarlet flowers attract wildlife. Lifespan variable. Needs moist sites.
Goldenrod *Solidago* spp.	N/C/S	M/Av/D	S/PSh	Four native species sold in Florida. Species depend on conditions. Yellow flowers, fall blooming. Does not cause hay fever.
Liatris *Liatris* spp.	N/C/S	M/Av/D	S	Four species available. Lavender, pinkish flowers borne on 2–4-foot spikes.
Purple Coneflower *Echinacea purpurea*	N/C	Av/D	S/PSh	Perennial with purple flowers. Extended bloom period. Requires well-drained soil.
Rain Lily *Zephyranthes atamasco*	N/C	M	PSh	Showy tubular white flowers after summer showers. Perennial.
Spider Lily *Hymenocallis latifolia*	SC/S	Av	S/PSh	Clump-forming perennial. Showy white petals with long golden anthers. Salt-tolerant.

Spiderwort *Tradescantia ohiensis*	N/C	M	S/PSh	Perennial blue or white flower. Spreads readily.
Stokes Aster *Stokesia laevis*	N/C	M	S/PSh	Perennial with showy lavender to bluish flowers. Attracts butterflies. Can spread.
String Lily *Crinum americanum*	N/C/S	M	S/PSh	Showy white flowers spring and summer. Can take wet conditions. Perennial.
Tickseed *Coreopsis leavenworthii*	N/C/S	M	S	Showy yellow flowers. Good butterfly attractor. Reseeding annual.
Tropical Sage *Salvia coccinea*	N/C/S	Av/D	S/PSh	Red-flowering annual. Reseeds prolifically. Attracts butterflies and hummingbirds.
Wild Petunia *Ruellia caroliniensis*	N/C/S	D/Av/M	S	Blue-flowering perennial. Reseeds.
Yellow Canna *Canna flaccida*	N/C/S	M	S/PSh	Bright yellow flowers. Can take standing water. Spreads vegetatively by underground stems.

Abbreviations: N (north) C (central) S (south) S (sun) Sh (shade) PSh (part shade) Av (average) M (moist) D (dry)

Pond Plants

Know the planting depths for individual species of pond plants you choose to plant. Table X includes this and other information about the most common pond plants.

Ponds plants grow quickly and form large clumps seemingly overnight. Buy just a few at a time. They are easy to divide and can be replanted into larger containers or given away to fellow pond-lovers.

Many will escape the containers in which you plant them and root amongst the accumulated leaf detritus and soil at the bottom of your pond. You will need to remove excessive vegetation every once in a while to keep plants from completely taking over.

Table X. Pond Plants

Abbreviations: N (north) C (central) S (south) S (sun) Sh (shade) PSh (part shade) Av (average) M (moist) D (dry)

Common Name *Botanical Name*	Range	Max Depth (inches)	Comment
Alligator Flag *Thalia geniculata*	N/C/S	48	Tall flower stalks. Large leaves with purplish flowers. Perennial dies back in the winter.
Arrowheads, Duck Potato *Sagittaria* spp.	N/C/S	18	Prefers inundation. White to bluish flowers. Four species available in Florida.
Blue-flag Iris *Iris virginica*	N/C	Edge	Showy blue flowers spring to summer. Spreads.
Bulrushes *Scirpus* spp.	N/C/S	12–36	Four Florida species. Seeds attract birds.
Horsetail *Equisetum hyemale*	N/C/S	36	Submerged pond plant. Perennial.
Lemon Bacopa *Bacopa caroliniana*	N/C/S	6	Six inches tall. Blue flowers. Mat-forming perennial. Can grow in ponds.
Fragrant Water Lily *Nymphaea odorata*	N/C/S	36	Perennial aquatic. Large fragrant white flowers and large floating leaves.

Pickerel Weed *Pontederia cordata*	N/C/S	24	Perennial aquatic. Tubular flowers. Blue with yellow markings. Grows rapidly and spreads.
Soft Rush *Juncus effusus*	N/C/S	6	Provides food and cover for wildlife. Clump-forming perennial.
Water Hyssop *Bacopa monnieri*	N/C/S	6	White to pinkish flowers. Mat-forming perennial. Can grow in ponds.
Yellow Canna *Canna flaccida*	N/C/S	12	Bright yellow flowers. Can take standing water. Spreads vegetatively by underground stems.

Ferns

Light and moisture tolerances vary amongst the native fern species. Some species grow well in moderately sunny, fairly dry to moist areas of your yard. Others prefer shady dry to wet spots. Others will do equally well in any of these conditions.

Some, such as the giant leather fern, will grow to eight feet tall and easily twelve to fifteen feet across. They grow in large V-shaped clumps. There are also smaller clump-growing ferns to choose from that range from three to six feet tall with an equal spread. Others grow as dense masses spreading their roots under or across the ground where conditions are favorable.

Plant ferns amongst shade-tolerant grasses for a naturalized, woodsy landscape. It is not necessary to fill every inch of space under trees or in shady areas. In nature, plant groupings are interspersed with areas of bare ground and leaf litter, although we recommend covering bare ground with mulch to control invasive weeds.

Native ferns can be aggressive and cover large areas quickly, but you can control their growth by pulling young individuals out as they spread from the original planting area. Intolerance to sun or drought also limits the spread of ferns in your yard.

Since ferns grow lushly and are deep green they add a tropical, cooling feel to your landscape. They also provide cover for wildlife, especially frogs and other amphibians. Ferns are easy to grow and transplant easily to other areas of your yard. Choose wisely to begin with, and future care will mostly involve decisions about how large an area you want them to fill.

Table XI. Ferns

Abbreviations: N (north) C (central) S (south) CS (south central) S (sun) Sh (shade) PSh (part shade) M (moist) W (wet) Fl (flooded)

Common Name *Botanical Name*	Range	Height (feet)	Light	Moisture	Comment
Boston Fern *Nephrolepis exaltata*	SC/S	1–3	PSh/Sh	M/W	Rapid aggressive growth. Spreads by underground rhizomes.
Cinnamon Fern *Osmunda cinnamomea*	N/C/S	2–4	Sh	M/W	Clump-forming. Showy fertile deciduous fronds.
Giant Sword Fern *Nephrolepis biserrata*	SC/S	3–5	PSh/Sh	M/W	Similar to Boston Fern but larger.
Leather Fern *Acrostichum danaeifolium*	SC/S	6–8	PSh	M/Fl	Large fern good for pond edges. Size makes it shrublike. Tolerates brackish water.

Royal Fern *Osmunda regalis*	N/C/S	2–5	S/Sh	M/W	Handsome fern that can tolerate wet sites. Clump-forming. Deciduous.
Virginia Chain Fern *Woodwardia virginica*	N/C/S	2–3	Sh/PSh	W/Fl	Showy perennial with colony-forming habit.

5

Selection,
Planting,
Establishment,
and Care

As a supplement to the material in this chapter we recommend two websites that contain more detailed information, including diagrams. One is posted by the International Society of Arboriculture (ISA) and the other by faculty members in the Environmental Horticulture Department at the University of Florida. Both websites are listed in the Resources section at the end of the book.

Selection

Make sure the plants you buy are healthy and growing vigorously. Check the foliage for evidence of major insect infestations such as scale, white-fly, or sooty mold. Leaves should be uniformly green. Check for damage to the trunk and major branches. Pull the plant out of the pot or stick your finger down into the pot and check for circling roots. Circling roots continue to circle once the plants are in the ground and can eventually strangle your tree or shrub. There should be numerous new, fine, white root hairs, which indicate the plant is growing vigorously. Avoid plants that have a mass of roots with very little visible soil. There should be only one tree or shrub in a container so there has been sufficient room for root growth.

Do not select plants that have been pruned to a ball shape, as they will never regain their natural form. Shrubs should have a pyramidal shape to allow sunlight to penetrate to the lowest branches. Woody individuals that have been severely pruned will have thick lower branches with many weaker upper shoots spreading in all directions. These shoots may be too weak to successfully support later branching.

Canopy trees should have been pruned to a single leader. We have hurricane-force winds in Florida, and a central, well-developed main trunk will withstand winds that will crack and break weaker multiple-leader canopy trees. The lower branches on the trunk should be present to create and nourish trunk taper. Look for branching all around the trunk and at well-spaced intervals to the upper branches.

It is better to buy a smaller but well-rooted tree or shrub rather than the largest individual you can find. Overgrown containerized plants may have too much foliage to be supported by their limited root mass. When these specimens are planted they require more water during the establishment period than plants with a proper balance between roots and shoots. This is particularly true for trees. Generally the longer the tree has been grown in a container, the longer it will take to get established in your yard.

Container-grown plants in Florida will be planted into predominately sandy soils. Consequently, plants that have been grown in a loose, porous, sandy potting soil are easier to establish than those grown in peat.

Planting

Dig the hole at least twice as wide as the container the plant has been grown in. This is especially important in poorly drained or compacted soils when you are planting trees that have been grown in fifteen-gallon or larger containers.

The planting hole should be no deeper than the depth of the root ball. Plant roots require oxygen. Planting too deeply is a major reason plants fail here in Florida. Sandy soils are easy to dig into so we often dig too deep a hole and then back-fill. If you do this, the plant may settle over time, the roots will become oxygen-deprived, and the plant will suffer. Digging in heavy clay soils or compacted soils requires much more effort so there is also a tendency to dig too deeply, thinking that this will give the plant roots loose soil in which to grow after you back-fill. Plant settling is also a problem under these conditions. We suggest you initially err on the side of too shallow a hole that you may need to make deeper before planting. After you plant, the surface roots that had been visible at the surface of the pot should be visible at the surface of the soil you plant into. In poorly drained soils, plant shallowly so that about a third of the containerized soil mass will be above the surrounding ground level. Cover the sides of the exposed root mass with soil. This will enable the plant to spread its roots out into soil that is not water-saturated.

Do not amend the planting hole with compost, manure, fertilizer, peat, or other enriching or water-retentive materials. This can retard the growth of the roots into the surrounding soil. After you place the plant upright in the hole, water the planting hole as you back-fill with soil. This will eliminate air pockets that can cause damage to the roots.

Remove all competing vegetation beneath newly planted trees and shrubs at least out to the drip line. Surrounding vegetation competes for moisture and nutrients with the newly planted material. Place a mounded ring of soil around the base of the planted tree at the edge of the root ball to hold water during the establishment period.

If you realize that your plant has sunk too deeply into the ground after planting, it may be advisable to replant it if it is young enough to survive the effort.

Trees that are in containers fifteen gallons or larger may need staking to prevent wind throw. Younger trees that are not staked will sway in the wind, but this will speed up anchoring root growth.

Mulch all new plantings. Mulch conserves moisture and reduces weeds, both of which are critical in Florida to successfully establish plants.

Mulch

Mulches come in many forms, both organic and inorganic. They vary from leaves, pine straw, chopped bark, recycled yard waste, newspapers, and peanut hulls to stones, lava rock, rubber, and shell. We recommend organic mulches. Stone and shell are better used for pathways and parking areas. Organic mulches keep the roots of newly planted vegetation cool and maintain soil moisture while plants are becoming established. They suppress weeds and break down slowly, providing humus and small quantities of natural fertilizer.

It doesn't really matter what type of organic mulch you use as long as you don't use the cheaper grade of cypress mulch. Living cypress trees are being logged out of swamps in the state's interior to be ground up and spread as mulch on coastal landscapes. Don't kill a tree to mulch a tree.

If you use commercially produced mulch, we recommend Florimulch produced from the melaleuca, or "punk" tree, which is available mostly in south central and south Florida. This tree was originally planted by the Army Corp of Engineers in the Everglades in the early 1920s as a way of drying up swamps. It is now a pest plant because it spreads rapidly to new areas and displaces native vegetation. Though it is now illegal to plant it in Florida, melaleuca still infests large areas of the Everglades. Using melaleuca mulch will help eliminate this invasive exotic. Additionally, it was rated the longest-lasting mulch by the University of Florida in a recent study of commonly used mulches. We find it does not float, is bug resistant, and suppresses weeds. We also recommend pine straw as excellent commercial mulch. It is lighter in weight than Florimulch, easier to handle, breaks down more quickly to provide humus to impoverished soils, and looks "woodsy."

Utilize what's on your own property when you can. If you rake leaves from your lawn, use them to mulch your plants. Live and laurel oak leaves, slash and longleaf pine needles, and leaves from other trees and shrubs in your yard make excellent mulch. That is the natural way of recycling nutrients from the roots to the growing shoot. Leaves and needles break down slowly and, over time, acidify the soil, which is advantageous to most plants.

Recycled mulch may also be available from county landfills and utility company tree trimmers who will drop off a load if they are in your area. Commercial mulches are fine but add to the cost of your garden projects. If you like its uniform look, you can save money by putting two to three inches of recycled mulch down first and top dress with commercial mulch.

Spread mulch at least three inches deep around your plants. Mulch out to the drip line of newly planted trees and shrubs, but keep the mulch six to eight inches away from tree trunks and stems of your shrubbery to avoid fungal and insect problems. Remember to spread it between plants because weeds grow wherever there is bare soil. Mulch heavily when you initially plant, and add to the existing mulch about every six months until weeds are only a minor nuisance. Spot applications of herbicide will be useful as weeds appear. As your plants mature they will compete with weeds for available nutrients, sunlight, and water.

Establishment

The establishment period is the time during which plants develop the ability to exist on rainfall. Plants grown under nursery conditions have been watered every day, perhaps twice a day in hotter weather. When you plant containerized flowers, shrubs, and trees, you must wean them from these conditions. Watering frequency and duration will differ depending on the season in which you plant. Late fall and winter months are less stressful because of lower air and soil temperatures.

Intense summer rainstorms can reduce the need for additional watering. A general suggestion is to begin watering every day for several weeks, then every other day for a few more weeks, then every third day. Watch for wilting of the outer leaves. Wilting at the end of the day is all right if it occurs in hot weather. Tip die-back caused by too little or infrequent watering will set your plants back. It will slow establishment and weaken physical and chemical defenses against insect, bacterial, fungal, and viral infestations.

Ideally the entire root ball should be saturated every time you water. It is better to water deeply and less frequently than frequently but shallowly. Determine if you have applied enough water by sticking your finger deep into the soil next to the root ball about an hour after you water. The soil should be moist as far as you can feel. This "finger test" is also a way to determine when you need to water again. You should water when the root ball is dry and not by some predetermined watering schedule.

The establishment period for smaller, younger plants will be shorter than for larger, more mature plants. The former may take two to three weeks while the latter may take two to three months. Trees and shrubs that you can take home in the trunk of your car, pickup truck, or van should be on their own at the end of their first growing season. Larger trees will take additional watering in the hot, dry months of their second year to become fully established.

Newly planted trees and shrubs may appear for some time as though they aren't growing, but they are producing the roots needed to support new shoot growth. Think of it this way: the first year they sleep, the second year they creep, the third year they leap. This is especially true in the long growing seasons here in Florida. Be patient. Your plants are established when they produce new growth without supplemental watering.

Care

Native plants have natural forms and growth rates that are determined by both their genetics and their environment. Their forms and growth rates will vary in response to environmental variables such as sunlight, soil moisture, and nutrients. If they are appropriately placed, they will thrive without our shaping, supplemental irrigation, added nutrients, and pest control. Realizing this from the start will make an important difference in your approach to caring for your native plants.

Pruning

Plant properly and you will have little pruning to do. Know approximately how tall and wide your plants will naturally grow. Don't crowd them up against walls or other surfaces or against each other. Space your plants so that at maturity they will have sunlight, air circulation, and root space. Plant far enough away from sidewalks, curbs, driveways, patios, and doors so that you will not have to brush against or duck beneath wet foliage. We tend to be impatient and try to fill all of the available planting space. Some initial patience will pay off in a few years when your properly spaced plants do well without extensive pruning.

There is one situation where pruning is necessary. Canopy trees require a strong main trunk (central leader) to withstand high winds. Florida No.1 trees will have a strong leader, but will need pruning as the tree matures. Your local Cooperative Extension Service should have articles on proper tree pruning methods; there are also books on the subject and information on the Web. Hire only certified arborists when your trees become too large for you to prune safely.

You may also want to prune "leggy" plants, but pruning is wounding. It exposes tender tissue to the elements as well as to fungal spores and insects that can introduce disease. Prune sparingly with some knowledge of the natural growth habit of each plant. Eliminate crossing branches, whips, and diseased or dead limbs. Always cut just above a growing node when pruning herbaceous plants and shrubs. Cut just outside the branch collar on tree branches.

The best times to prune are at the end of winter, mid-summer, and early fall. Don't prune nondormant plants during the winter months because pruning stimulates new growth, which may be injured by cold nights or freezing temperatures.

Fertilizing

It may seem intuitive that plants growing in a sandy soil need added nutrients, but native plants can thrive in most soils without added fertilizer, unlike turf grass, fruit trees, and some exotic flowering plants and vegetables. The slow decomposition of leaf litter over time, in combination with the accumulation of windblown detritus, has been sufficient to sustain natives in natural areas.

If native plants don't thrive where you have planted them, the limiting factors are most likely to be pH, salinity, or an excess or lack of soil moisture and sun. Fertilizer has little or no effect on these soil or environmental conditions. If you still suspect a nutritional problem, take a leaf into your Cooperative Extension office for their opinion.

If you have eliminated all other possibilities for the poor health of your plants and the County Extension folks think your leaves show signs of nutrient deficiencies, then fertilize. When you do, use slow-release pellet fertilizers that only release nutrients when moistened. Organic fertilizers, with low levels of nutrients, are also a good alternative to quick-release, broad-spectrum fertilizers. The latter readily dissolve and their components often sink quickly below available roots or escape down storm drains into local waterways. Pruning and fertilization will cause flushes of new growth that will be susceptible to attack by leaf-sucking insects. These in turn can introduce fungal and viral diseases into plants.

If you must fertilize, do it after the last winter frost date for your area. Late fall fertilization can encourage tender new growth that is susceptible to low temperatures. Spring rains, warmer days and nights, and longer days naturally trigger new growth at this time and your plants will utilize fertilizer more readily. Another good time is before the beginning of our rainy season, around mid-June. Again, plants will respond to frequent and abundant rainfall in addition to long, warm days and nights. These fertilization suggestions are valid for your non-native plants as well as any natives.

If you have turf grass and want it to look good you will need to fertilize. Before you fertilize you should have the soil tested to determine the levels of nitrogen, phosphorus, and potassium. Some Florida soils are rich in phosphorus; the addition of phosphorus should be minimized if that is the case for your soil. It is best to use a slow-release fertilizer containing water-insoluble nitrogen. The University of Florida recommends a maximum of 0.5 lb of soluble nitrogen/1000ft^2 of lawn. A good place to look for more detailed lawn fertilizer recommendations for your area is at your local Cooperative Extension Office or on the University of Florida website.

Insects

Plant pest problems are often the result of planting the wrong plant in the wrong place. Plants under stress are more susceptible to pests. Look for underlying problems such as too much or too little water, too much or too little sun, crowding, planting too deeply, and mechanical injury to the roots or support structure. Rule out these factors before you think about pest management. All plants are subject to visits by insects whether or not they are natives. If that were not so, insect-eating birds would starve and many plants would not be pollinated. In most cases the visits do minimal damage to the plants. Learn to ignore them. If you feel compelled to act, the least intrusive methods are picking off insects, hosing them off, and pruning infected material. As a last resort, use insecticidal oils or soaps that are relatively safe to humans and higher life forms. But know that chemical sprays, including soaps and oils, will kill beneficial insects as well as pests, not to mention butterflies and other benign and attractive insects.

Planting a variety of plants in your yard creates niches for many different kinds of beneficial insects. These are insects that parasitize and kill insect pests. Let them become part of your local food web and respond to pest infestations by preying on pest species.

Disease

Native plants are subject to a variety of diseases caused by fungi, bacteria, and viruses, although they are rarely infected if the plants are properly placed and planted. Most diseases do relatively little damage to the plant, although they can be aesthetically displeasing. In the latter category are some of the leaf spot diseases, which are probably the most common type of fungal disease. One way to minimize the occurrence of these diseases is to space plants properly to allow for proper air circulation.

Sooty mold is a fungal disease that leads to a nonlethal black deposit on leaves. The cause of this disease is usually the honeydew left by aphids and other insects. If you have sooty mold on a plant you should inspect it for insect infestations. If a tree shows sign of branch die-back or if there are mushroomlike growths on or around the tree, you should consult a Florida-certified arborist or talk to your local Cooperative Extension personnel. If a plant dies for no apparent reason it is best not to replant the same species in the same location.

Plant a variety of plants in your yard to create niches for many different kinds of beneficial insects. Let them become part of your local food web and respond to pest infestations by preying on pest species. This is the approach you should take to control plant pest problems. Rather than using pesticides, either relocate or eliminate problematic plantings.

6
Environmental
Challenges

Sun/Shade

In Florida, unlike in many other parts of the country, most plants do well in partial shade. Dune and scrub plants, aquatic plants, and those growing in wetland prairies are the only plants that naturally grow in full sun. In all other natural areas, dominant tree species at least partially shade understory and ground cover plants. This includes pine flatwoods, oak and palm woodlands, coastal hammocks, and cypress swamps. If you visit these habitats you will see that even in very open woodlands the scattered tall trees provide some shade for at least part of the day.

Most understory plants can grow in full sun but may do better in light shade. For this reason you can plant your trees and understory at the same time. The understory plants will survive and adapt over time to the increasing shade provided by your trees. Where you don't have room for trees, tall shrubs will also provide some shade for smaller shrubs and ground covers.

Pines provide ideal conditions for understory plants since they provide a high, light shade. The shade of oaks and deciduous trees is often deeper. Watch how shade changes over the course of the day and plant where some sun filters down through the canopy at least part of the day. Deep shade cast by dense tree groupings or closely packed smaller trees and shrubs may limit plant selection but there are natives that will grow in these conditions too.

The south and west sides of your home are the sunniest and growing conditions there are harshest. Plants growing there must tolerate long hours of sun, including the searing late-afternoon sun. Make sure the plants you choose for those areas can take full sun. Morning sun on the east and north sides is not as harsh.

The winter sun is lower in the sky so that shade extends over different areas of your yard for differing periods than it does in summer months. Shade cast by your house also changes throughout the year. This means that in one part of the year areas of your yard may be in shade while they are in the sun during other months. Not all plants can take a change from winter shade to the full sun of summer. Choose plants for these areas that can tolerate a wide range of light conditions.

It is not necessary to cover the ground with plants in intense sun or very shady conditions. In nature there are often large open areas where the ground is covered with leaf litter with an occasional tuft of native grass or isolated patch of wildflowers or vine. If conditions are too sunny and harsh, or too shady, you might think about mulching instead of planting these places. Place a sculpture, pond, fountain, pathway, or sitting area where plants grow only with great difficulty.

Table XII. Plants for Full Sun and Deep Shade

Full Sun		Deep shade	
Beach Plants		Shrubs	Palms
Coontie		Anise	Sabal Palm
Grasses		Beautyberry	Needle Palm
Saw Palmetto		Coral Bean	Saw Palmetto
		Firebush	
		Marlberry	Vines
		Myrsine	Corky Stem Passion Vine
		Pinxter Azalea	Cross Vine
		Pipestem	
		Stoppers	Miscellaneous
		Wild Coffee	Coontie
			Ferns
			Gamma Grass

Poorly Drained Sites

Most of Florida, except for the coast and central ridge, was once part of the most common plant community in the southeast, called the pine flatwoods. It is characterized by acidic sandy soil that commonly has a hardpan layer one to three feet below the surface. This hardpan layer, which is highly impervious to water, causes the lower-lying surface soils to be saturated or even to pool water during the summer rainy season. A few days of these conditions can kill plants that are not adapted to them.

This problem is exacerbated where new homes are elevated above the local flood plain. Water running off from the elevated sites can cause drainage problems for surrounding properties. Construction of berms and swales to redirect and/or hold storm water can also create poorly drained areas in your yard or in your neighbor's yard.

In wetter summers we see the results caused by these drainage problems. Such a season provides ample opportunities to inspect your property for the areas that are particularly prone to saturated or flooded soils. Don't modify your property by filling in or mounding low spots. Take advantage of these areas by incorporating plants that are adapted to flooding, but can also tolerate the dry conditions that may exist for much of the year. Native plants are particularly useful in this respect because a number of them have adapted to the ephemeral wet/dry conditions that occur in our state. You could also take advantage of wet areas by creating a pond. Ponds provide another way to increase plant diversity and attract wildlife.

Wet ground can be a plus in your landscape. It allows you to increase your plant diversity and add interest to your yard. If the water table is near or at the surface for much of the year, you can plant wetland species such as soft-stem bulrush, blue-flag iris, yellow canna lilies, and various cordgrasses. Bald cypress, maples, sweet gum, and sweet bay magnolia all thrive in wetter soils inland. Along the coast, both silver and green buttonwood do well in wetter areas. Wetland shrubs such as wax myrtle, sweet spire, Florida privet, coastal willow, Walter's viburnum, buttonbush, and elderberry will create a different aesthetic and draw birds that frequent freshwater wetlands. The sides of wet swales, so often filled with dead or dying turf grasses, can be planted with native clump grasses that do very well and look lovely, or low-growing mimosa that survives inundation for a few days at a time.

If your yard is wet, smile and enjoy it. Don't try to alter your growing place. Instead alter your plant composition using some of the plants in Table XIII. Learn to enjoy dragonflies.

Table XIII. Plants for Poorly Drained Sites

Trees	Shrubs	Ferns	Flowers
American Elm	Buttonbush	Cinnamon Fern	Blue-flag Iris
Bald Cypress	Virginia Willow	Leather Fern	Yellow Canna
Buttonwood		Royal Fern	Spiderwort
Dahoon Holly		Sword Fern	Rain Lily
Green Ash			Cardinal Flower
Loblolly Bay			
Laurel Oak			
Pond Apple			
Red Maple			
River Birch			

Well-drained Sites

Well-drained means those areas of your yard that appear dry twenty minutes after a heavy storm. By plants for well-drained sites, we mean the plants that flourish in the sunniest, hottest, highest, and driest parts of your yard. You might think high and dry refers to all of your property but it probably doesn't. Elevations are subtle here, sometimes very subtle. Inches can make a difference in drainage patterns and where rainfall accumulates on your property after a summer storm. Your house foundation is elevated above the surrounding flood plain, and water drains off it toward a stormwater drain or retention pond.

Well-drained areas require plant groupings that can tolerate dry to very dry conditions, particularly in the spring months when it can be both hot and dry. Typically, humus doesn't accumulate in well-drained areas either, so that these areas are high, dry, and nutrient-poor.

There are plants that thrive in these conditions. Some grow in dry, sunny conditions while others require at least some respite from the sun. Dry conditions almost all the time is the unifying factor. In fact, many dry land plants survive only in these conditions. They rot if inundated and succumb to fungal diseases if grown in rich soils or smothered in mulch.

Plants for well-drained sites should be grouped together on your property. Start with trees and shrubs that thrive under these conditions and add clump grasses and wildflowers beneath and around them. Obviously, these plants will require some additional watering to get established, but when they no longer wilt in the late afternoon, stop watering them. There may also be times where additional water may be required during their first year. Dry land shrubs and trees need more time to grow sufficient roots to support growth. This is especially true of larger trees that might require two or three growing seasons to become established. We recommend planting younger trees and shrubs in areas that are well-drained as they will require less watering to become established.

Table XIV. Plants for Well-Drained Sites

Trees	Shrubs	Grasses	Palms/ Coonties	Flowers	Ground Covers
Chickasaw Plum	Adam's Needle	Elliott's Love Grass	Brittle Thatch Palm	Blanket Flower	Golden Creeper
Gumbo Limbo	Fiddlewood	Muhly Grass	Coontie	Beach Dune Sunflower	Gopher Apple
Live Oak	Sea Grape	Sea Oats	Saw Palmetto		Railroad Vine
Longleaf Pine	Wild Sage		Scrub Palmetto		Beach Elder
Myrtle Oak	Yaupon Holly				
Red Cedar					

Trees					
Sand Live Oak					
Slash Pine					
Sweet Acacia					
Wild Tamarind					
Winged Elm					

Cold

Many folks who come to Florida from the North assume that we live in a tropical climate where cold and frost don't have to be taken into consideration when planting. This is usually the case for south Florida (USDA Zones 10A, 10B, and 11) where freezing temperatures are rare, although they do occur, particularly in the more interior areas of 10A. Only the lower Keys in Zone 11 can truly be said to be frost-free. In north Florida (Zones 8A and B) one learns quickly that you can expect winter mornings when the temperatures dip into the high teens or low twenties, and you must plant accordingly. In central Florida (9A and 9B) there are relatively warm winters (average lows in January are around 50° but we can usually expect at least one early morning of below-freezing temperatures. In some winters there are no such days, while in other winters there may be two or three. Occasionally, when a particularly powerful "Alberta clipper" arrives there will be temperatures sufficiently low to damage or kill most plants that are not cold-hardy, even in central Florida. Plants that are native to your area will rarely suffer from the cold, but even plants that are native to Florida but not to your area can be damaged if they are not cold-hardy.

Crucial to this analysis is the location of your house, because during cold spells there is usually a temperature gradient from the coast inland. It is clear that the USDA zones are really not sufficiently localized to cover all the temperature variations and can be used only as a general guideline. At our nursery fifteen miles east of Sarasota, the temperature may be six or seven degrees lower than is experienced by someone living on one of the barrier islands.

Although slightly below freezing for a few hours doesn't sound terribly stressful, many tropical plants will suffer damage ranging from loss of leaves and die-back of twigs to death. Most plants that you see flowering in December or January fit this category.

When you purchase plants for your landscape you should be aware of their cold-hardiness, particularly plants that are perennial and that you hope to have for a number of years. Of course, you may be willing to gamble on a cold-sensitive plant because you particularly like its appearance. If you do, try to plant it close to the southeast corner of your house and surround it with more cold-hardy plants. Also be prepared to cover it when temperatures are scheduled to drop. Talk to knowledgeable gardeners in your area about their experiences, as well as to the people from whom you buy your plants. You can save yourself trouble, however, by installing plants that are quite cold-hardy. This is especially important when considering trees for your property. Trees are a long-term investment. It takes time to get them established and money to provide the maintenance necessary to create a healthy canopy. Cold damage to trees can be devastating. Cold-sensitive trees can suffer branch rot after a severe frost, which can eventually involve the trunk and cause damage all the way down into the base of tree. This will compromise its structure and may require that you pay to have the tree cut down and hauled away. This can be very expensive, particularly if it is a sizable tree near your home or in a part of the yard where it will be hard to reach. There are many native trees and shrubs that are cold-hardy (see Tables I, II, III, IV). Most of them naturally range into north Florida where they are often subjected to temperatures in the high teens or low twenties.

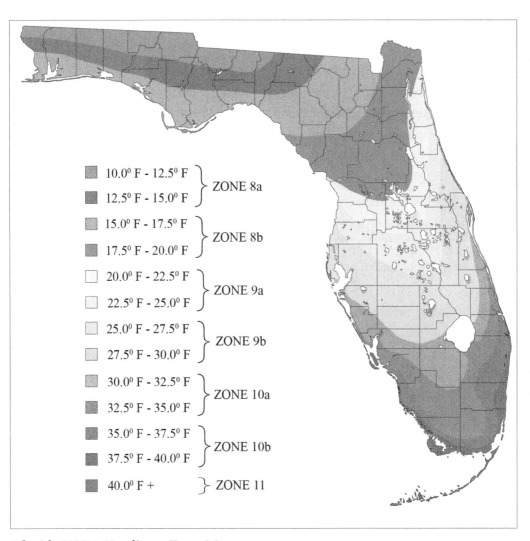

10.0⁰ F - 12.5⁰ F	
	ZONE 8a
12.5⁰ F - 15.0⁰ F	
15.0⁰ F - 17.5⁰ F	
	ZONE 8b
17.5⁰ F - 20.0⁰ F	
20.0⁰ F - 22.5⁰ F	
	ZONE 9a
22.5⁰ F - 25.0⁰ F	
25.0⁰ F - 27.5⁰ F	
	ZONE 9b
27.5⁰ F - 30.0⁰ F	
30.0⁰ F - 32.5⁰ F	
	ZONE 10a
32.5⁰ F - 35.0⁰ F	
35.0⁰ F - 37.5⁰ F	
	ZONE 10b
37.5⁰ F - 40.0⁰ F	
40.0⁰ F +	ZONE 11

Florida USDA Hardiness Zone Map.

This map is derived from NOAA data and the Plant Hardiness Zone Map published by the United States Department of Agriculture.

Coastal/Salt

If you live on or very near the beach, choose salt-tolerant native plants for your landscape. Salt-tolerant is a broad term that describes plants that can thrive in places subject to salt spray, salt water inundation, or salt water intrusion into shallow wells used for irrigation.

Three general beach areas require different levels of salt-tolerance in plants. The frontal zone extends from the high-tide line to areas of the beach in which the sand is stable. Native grasses and trailing vines do well here and are the only plants that can handle the salt spray and drifting sand. The back dune, where the sand is stable, supports a select group of native salt-tolerant trees, shrubs, and other herbaceous plants as well as native grasses and vines. Farthest from the beach is the forest zone where pines and oaks and other hardwoods grow.

If you have shoreline and want to plant on the bare sands of the frontal zone, choose sand-colonizing plants (see Table XV). Plants in this zone must be able to tolerate shifting sand and salt spray. Salt-tolerant grass species and creeping, colonizing vines thrive in this zone.

Very few native trees and shrubs do well just shoreward of the frontal zone into the back zone. This is still a tough area for plants. Sands are fairly stable here but salt spray is still intense since there is no buffer between these plants and winds blowing off the water. Further inland into the back zone, where wind and salt spray are not constant, sabal palm, sea grape (south Florida), and sand live oak (north Florida) will grow. These are the only shade-providing trees for this area of the beach. Tropical storms, however, can still cause considerable damage to plants in this area.

Sabal palms planted in clusters of five to seven individuals will shade patios and sitting areas located on back dunes and further inland. They are inexpensive and transplant easily. Choose individuals of varying heights for a natural look. They are cold-hardy and are probably the most hurricane-resistant plants in Florida.

Sea grapes make wonderful small trees. They can grow to twenty-five feet tall and provide dense shade. You can remove the lower branches and allow the upper canopy to grow either as a single trunk or a multi-trunked tree. The leaves will turn orange-brown and fall off after being buffeted with salt-laden air from a storm, but the plant refoliates quickly. This is not the ideal plant for open pool areas, but in other areas fallen leaves make a long-lasting mulch.

Sand live oak is a shrubby evergreen tree. It has shiny, dark–green, leathery leaves and gnarled branches. You can intersperse it with palms to create a more natural look.

Shrubs adapted to this area of the beach, such as yaupon holly, will most likely be stunted and shaped by wind and salt spray into interesting configurations. During storms they may lose their leaves, but will refoliate. Plants unable to withstand such conditions will not survive.

In the forest zone a variety of plants grow well (see Table XV). It is an area where dune plants, coastal species, and inland species intermix.

Other areas that require salt-tolerant plants are the land sides of sea walls and the banks of tidal brackish creeks. Plants in these areas can occasionally be flooded by brackish water, and you need to choose plants that can survive salt water inundation (see Table XV).

Another problem that is becoming more common is salt water intrusion into shallow wells. Folks who live in coastal areas and who use shallow well water to irrigate their plants should have their water tested for salt levels. If you do have salt water intrusion, then you should stop using well water for irrigation unless you have salt-tolerant plants. Since even native plants require watering until they are acclimated, native plants that don't tolerate a moderate level of salt will not do well.

No section on salt-tolerant coastal plants would be complete without reference to mangrove trees. They grow naturally along the edges of saline bays and tidal streams. Mangroves are protected at the federal, state, and local levels in Florida, and the state and many local municipalities regulate mangrove trimming. Protect natural stands of mangroves on your property. Don't hedge mangroves to a six foot height as currently allowed in many counties, since you will eliminate habitat for shoreline wildlife by doing this. A more environmentally sensitive approach is to remove only select branches in order to create desirable views.

Table XV. Salt-Tolerant Plants

Abbreviations: FD (front dunes) BD (back dunes) FL (flooded) FZ (forest zone)

Trees	Zones		Grasses	Zones
Buttonwood	FL		Muhly Grass	BD, BL
Geiger Tree	FZ		Salt Meadow Cordgrass	FD, FL
Gumbo Limbo	FZ		Sand Cordgrass	BD, FL
Jamaica Caper	FZ		Sea Oats	FD
Live Oak	FZ			
Mahogany	FZ			
Longleaf Pine	FZ		Ground covers	Zones
Mastic	FZ		Golden Creeper	BD
Myrtle Oak	FZ		Railroad Vine	FD
Pigeon Plum	FZ		Wild Plumbago	FZ
Sand Live Oak	BD, FZ			
Slash Pine	FZ			
Sweet Acacia	FZ			
Wild Tamarind	FZ			
Shrubs	Zones		Palms/Coontie	Zones
Adam's Needle	FZ		Brittle Thatch Palm	FZ
Bahama Senna	FZ		Sabal Palm	BD, FL, FZ
Beautyberry	FZ		Coontie	FZ
Christmas Berry	FL		Saw Palmetto	FZ

Coral Bean	FZ		Wildflowers	Zones
Cocoplum	FL		Beach Dune Sunflower	BD, FD
Florida Privet	FL, FZ		Blanket Flower	BD
Marlberry	FZ		Seaside Goldenrod	BD, FD
Myrsine	FL, FZ		Spider Lily	FL
Red Bay	FZ			
Sea Grape	BD, FZ			
Sea Oxeye	BD, FL			
Beach Elder	FD		Ferns	Zones
Stoppers	FZ		Leather Fern	FL
Wax Myrtle	FL, FZ			
Wild Coffee	FZ			
Wild Sage	FZ			
Yaupon Holly	FZ			
Mangroves	Zones			
Red, Black, White	FL			

Invasive Exotics

The Florida Exotic Pest Plant Council has defined the following terms:

Exotic—a species introduced to Florida, purposefully or accidentally, from a natural range outside of Florida.

Native—a species whose natural range included Florida at the time of European contact (1500 A.D.).

Invasive Exotic—an exotic that not only has naturalized but is expanding on its own in Florida plant communities.

There are two main causes of native habitat loss. One is development and the other is displacement by invasive exotics. The second type of loss may not be so obvious to most of us, but it is important. Native plants and animals have evolved together over thousands of years, so the loss of native plants reduces the food and shelter on which animals depend.

Without your permission invasive exotics leave your yard as seed on the wind, in water, as undigested material from birds and mammals, or even on your pants leg or the sole of your shoe. Once established in natural areas, invasive exotics are able to grow and reproduce at the expense of natives and, as a result, reduce biodiversity. In the worst cases, the native vegetation dies out, leaving an exotic monoculture. Instead of the diversity of native plant species supporting a variety of organisms, one exotic plant thrives and supports far fewer organisms. Once they become established, invasive exotics are very hard to eliminate. Millions of dollars have been spent in Florida during the past few years removing them from parks and other natural areas.

Not all exotics are invasive. Noninvasive exotics come from parts of the world other than Florida, but remain contained in the area in which they are planted. Since not all exotics are invasive, find out which ones are. The Florida Exotic Pest Plant Council on the Web at www.fleppc.org/ is one good source for information about invasive plants in your region. Your local Cooperative Extension office will also have publications about invasive exotics in your county and eradication methods.

You may be surprised to find out what shrubs and ground covers are invasive in your area. Surinam cherry, heavenly bamboo, sword fern, Mexican petunia, beach naupaka, schefflera, and seaside mahoe are but a few of the readily available, sought-after garden center invasive exotics. Many of our common ground covers such as oyster plant, grandmother's tongue, white-flowered wandering Jew, asparagus fern, or wedelia are also invasive exotics.

Obviously, large invasive trees like Australian pine, melaleuca (punk tree), and carrotwood are too big to remove yourself. Call in professionals, get quotes, and make sure whomever you choose is insured. Brazilian pepper, if they are medium-size trees or smaller, can be cut down by the homeowner. If these trees are your only form of shade, or buffer undesirable views, you can plant native replacements near them. As your replacements mature, you can cut back and slowly remove the exotics.

Nonwoody invasive exotic plants are more numerous than their woody counterparts and are just as harmful to the environment. They should all be removed and replaced with native plants.

Resources

Websites

Atlas of Florida Vascular Plants
www.plantatlas.usf.edu

Association of Florida Native Nurseries
www.afnn.org

Backyard Habitats and Ponds
http://edis.ifas.ufl.edu/FA037

Butterfly Gardening in Florida
http://edis.ifas.ufl.edu/UW057

Florida Backyard Wildlife Habitat Program
http://www.wec.ufl.edu/extension/

Florida Exotic Pest Plant Council
www.fleppc.org

Florida Native Plant Society
www.fnps.org

Florida-Friendly Yards
www.swfwmd.state.fl.us/yards

International Society of Arboriculture
www.treesaregood.com

Selection and Planting Trees and Shrubs
http://edis.ifas.ufl.edu/MG077

Books

Florida's Best Native Landscape Plants, 200 Readily Available Species. Gil Nelson. University Press of Florida, 2003.

Florida Butterfly Gardening. Marc C. Minno and Maria Minno. University Press of Florida, 1999.

Florida's Wildflowers in Their Native Communities. Walter Kingsley Taylor. University Press of Florida, 1998.

A Gardener's Guide to Florida Native Plants. Rufino Osorio. University Press of Florida, 2001.

Landscaping for Florida's Wildlife. Joe Schaefer and George Tanner. University Press of Florida, 1998.

Native Florida Plants, Low-Maintenance Landscaping and Gardening. Robert G. Haehle and Joan Brookwell. Taylor Trade Publishing, 2004.

Priceless Florida. Ellie Whitney, D. Bruce Means, and Anne Rudloe. Pineapple Press, 2004.

The Shrubs and Woody Vines of Florida. Gil Nelson. Pineapple Press, 1996.

The Trees of Florida. Gil Nelson. Pineapple Press, 1994.

Index

Notes

Here are some other books from Pineapple Press on related topics. For a complete catalog, write to Pineapple Press, P.O. Box 3889, Sarasota, Florida 34230-3889, or call (800) 746-3275. Or visit our website at www.pineapplepress.com.

The Art of South Florida Gardening, 2nd edition by Harold Songdahl and Coralee Leon. Gardening advice specifically written for the unique conditions of south Florida. This practical, comprehensive guide, written with humor and know-how, will teach you how to outsmart the soil, protect against pests and weather, and select the right trees and shrubs for Florida's climate.

Florida's Best Fruiting Plants by Charles R. Boning. A comprehensive guide to fruit-bearing plants that thrive in the Florida environment. Discusses exotics and native species, familiar plants, and dozens of rare and obscure plants.

100 Orchids for Florida by Jack Kramer. 100 beautiful orchids you can grow in Florida, chosen for their beauty, ease of cultivation, and suitability to Florida's climate.

Groundcovers for the South by Marie Harrison. Presents a variety of plants that can serve as groundcovers in the American South. Each entry gives detailed information on ideal growing conditions, plant care, and different selections within each species. Color photographs and line drawings make identification easy.

Southern Gardening: An Environmentally Sensitive Approach by Marie Harrison. A comprehensive guide to beautiful, environmentally conscious yards and gardens. Suggests useful groundcovers and easy-care, adaptable trees, shrubs, perennials, and annuals.

Gardening in the Coastal South by Marie Harrison. A Master Gardener discusses topics such as salt-tolerance, pesticide use, beneficial insects, invasive exotics, and gardening for butterflies and birds. Color photos and pen-and-ink illustrations round out the text.

Flowering Trees of Florida by Mark Stebbins. Written for both the seasoned arborist and the weekend gardener alike, this comprehensive guide offers 74 outstanding tropical flowering trees that will grow in Florida's subtropical climate. Full-color photos throughout.